About The

Three Nephites

"Therefore, more blessed are ye, for ye shall never taste of death."

(3 Nephi 28:7)

About The

Three
Nephites

C. Douglas Beardall
Jewel N. Beardall

LDS BOOK PUBLICATIONS
P. O. Box 1515
Provo, Utah 84603-1515
(801) 226-3539

Copyright © 1992 by C. Douglas Beardall
Published by LDS Book Publications
Box 1515, Provo, Utah 84603

Printed in the United States of America
ISBN: 1-882371-25-9

iv

Go, Ye Messengers of Glory

"Go, ye messengers of glory;
    Run, ye legates of the skies;
Go and tell the pleasing story,
    That a glorious angel flies;

    Great and mighty,
With a message from the skies.

"Go to every tribe and nation,
    Visit every land and clime;
Sound to all the proclamation;
    Tell to all the truth sublime:

    That the gospel
Does in ancient glory shine.

"Go, to all the gospel carry;
    Let the joyful news abound;
Go till every nation hears you,
    Jew and Gentile greet the
sound;
    Let the gospel
Echo all the earth around.

"Bearing seed of heavenly virtue,
    Scatter it o'er all the earth;
Go! Jehovah will support you,
    Gather all the sheaves of
worth,
    Then, with Jesus,
Reign in glory on the earth."

— President John Taylor

Preface

Our intent in gathering and compiling this wondrous collection of experiences and testimonies has a dual purpose. First, as a means of dispelling some of the rumors and myths which circulate from time to time. An experience which occurred in the early part of the century will be shared and passed around from one person to the next until it seldom is even similar to the original. This publication will help preserve the original words of the original experience in order to quash rumor and untruth.

Secondly, we wanted to produce a simple source book and reference where one could turn to for most of the well known experiences, and for some of the newer testimonies of the present day existence of the Three Nephites. By gathering together most of the previously published stories which have appeared in numerous publications, the reader is able to have easy access to study and enjoy these miraculous visitations of the ancient disciples.

Except for the quoting of actual scriptural references, these related experiences are not always meant to be doctrinal in nature, and may not always be sanctioned by The Church of Jesus Christ of Latter-day Saints. They are presented to you solely for the benefit of spiritual enhancement and righteous motivation. To uplift and inspire.

With an open and receptive heart, you might want to imagine that you are attending a "special testimony meeting" where those individuals who have experienced a visitation of the Three Nephites have been invited to share their personal testimonies with you. After all, this is probably the closest any of the rest of us will ever get to actually having the experiences ourselves.

C. Douglas Beardall
Jewel N. Beardall
— Provo, Utah —

Other book
Publications by
Douglas and Jewel Beardall—

For Missionaries Only!
The Qualities of Love
Death and the LDS Family
Latter-day Bondage
The Miracle of Love
Passage to Light
Cookbook for All Seasons
The Missionary Kit
Mormon Money Matters

I feel sorry for the man or woman who has never experienced the sweet joy which comes to the missionary who proclaims the Gospel of Jesus Christ, and brings honest souls to a knowledge of the truth, and who hears the expressions of gratitude and thanksgiving that come from the hearts of those who have been brought by his labor to a comprehension of life eternal. (*CR*, Oct. 1907, p.23)

—Heber J. Grant

This work is dedicated
to all those who love
to search the scriptures
for the plain and simple
truths found therein.

CONTENTS

Chapter   Page

Introduction

In finishing His initial work among the Nephites, Jesus appeared to the multitude for the third time and also to the twelve disciples whom He had chosen to lead. We know little of what actually happened as He ministered to the multitudes of the Nephites during His last visitation to them. The Book of Mormon records state that babes uttered marvelous things but that the people were forbidden to write those wonderful miracles which occurred.

As we read in 3 Nephi 19:4, the Twelve Disciples were each identified by name. The actual names of the Three Nephites is unknown to us today, but we are assured they are among these Twelve. Verse 4 reads as follows: "And it came to pass that on the morrow, when the multitude was gathered together, behold, Nephi and his brother whom he had raised from the dead, whose name was Timothy, and also his son, whose name was Jonas, and also Mathoni, and Mathonihah, his brother, and Kumen, and Kumenonhi, and Jeremiah, and

Shemnon, and Jonas, and Zedekiah, and Isaiah — now these were the names of the disciples whom Jesus had chosen — and it came to pass that they went forth and stood in the midst of the multitude." The Prophet Mormon wrote, "Behold, I was about to write the names of those who were never to taste of death, but the Lord forbade; therefore I write them not, for they are hid from the world. But behold, I have seen them, and they have ministered unto me." *(3 Nephi 28:25-26.)*

Jesus appeared to His disciples later and instructed them in many spiritual matters. "And it came to pass when Jesus had said these words, He spake unto His disciples, one by one, saying unto them: What is it that ye desire of me, after that I am gone to the Father?"

"And they all spake, save it were three, saying: We desire that after we have lived unto the age of man, that our ministry, wherein thou hast called us, may have an end, that we may speedily come unto thee in the kingdom."

"And He said unto them: Blessed are ye because ye desired this thing of me; therefore, after that ye are seventy and two years old ye shall come unto me in my kingdom; and with me ye shall find rest."

And when He had spoken unto them, He turned Himself unto the three, and said unto them: What will ye that I should do unto you, when I am gone unto the Father?"

"And they sorrowed in their hearts, for they

durst not speak unto Him the thing which they desired."

"And He said unto them: Behold, I know your thoughts, and ye have desired the thing which John, my beloved, who was with me in my ministry, before that I was lifted up by the Jews, desired of me."

"Therefore, more blessed are ye, for ye shall never taste of death; but ye shall live to behold all the doings of the Father unto the children of men, even until all things shall be fulfilled according to the will of the Father, when I shall come in my glory with the powers of heaven."

"And ye shall never endure the pains of death; but when I shall come in my glory ye shall be changed in the twinkling of an eye from mortality to immortality; and then shall ye be blessed in the kingdom of my Father."

"And again, ye shall not have pain while ye shall dwell in the flesh, neither sorrow save it be for the sins of the world; and all this will I do because of the thing which ye have desired of me, for ye have desired that ye might bring the souls of men unto me, while the world shall stand." *(3 Nephi 28:1-9.)*

Jesus granted the Three Nephites their common wish and desire, that they should "never taste of death." The Prophet Mormon, commenting on this promise over 300 years later, wrote that he had seen and talked with the Three Nephites, and that they had performed a mission of love among the Nephite people. Explaining the future work of the Three Nephites, Mormon said that they would labor among the Jews and Gentiles, but that they would not be recognized as the three special disciples. They were commanded by Jesus to minister to future generations, into the latter days, until the millennium of time.

In Mormon Doctrine, Elder Bruce R. McConkie clarifies that the Three Nephites "were to minister, as the angels of God, unto the Jews, Gentiles, scattered tribes of Israel, and unto all nations, kindreds, tongues, and people" as recorded in Third Nephi. Elder McConkie further states regarding the Three Nephites that, "unbeknowns to the world, they are continuing their assigned ministry at this time, and there have been occasions when they have appeared to members of the Church in this final dispensation." *(Mormon Doctrine, by Bruce R. McConkie. Bookcraft, 1966. pg. 793.)*

Elder James E. Talmage wrote in his book, "Jesus the Christ, A Study of the Messiah and His Mission", about the three by saying, "A change was wrought in the bodies of the Three Nephites, so that, while they remained in the flesh, they were exempt from the usual effects of physical vicissitude. Though they lived and labored as men among their fellows, preaching, baptizing, and conferring the Holy Ghost upon all who gave heed to their words, the enemies to the truth were powerless to do them injury."

"Somewhat later than a hundred and seventy years after the Lord's last visitation, malignant persecution was waged against the Three. For their zeal in the ministry they were cast into prison but 'the prisons could not hold them, for they were rent in twain'. They were incarcerated in underground dungeons; 'But they did smite the earth with the word of God, insomuch that by his power they were delivered out of the depths of the earth; and therefore they could not dig pits sufficient to hold them'."

"Thrice they were cast into a furnace of fire, but received no harm; and three times were they thrown into dens of ravenous beasts, but, 'behold they did play with the beasts, as a child with a suckling lamb, and received no harm'." *(3 Nephi 28:19-22.)*

"Mormon avers that in answer to his prayers the Lord had made known unto him that the change wrought upon the bodies of the Three, was such as to deprive Satan of all power over them, and that 'they were holy, and that the powers of the earth could not hold them; and in this state they were to remain until the judgment day of Christ; and at that day they were to receive a greater change, and to be received into the kingdom of the Father to go no more out, but to dwell with God eternally in the heavens'. *(3 Nephi 28:39-40.)* The blessed Three were assured that in the course of their prolonged life they should be immune to pain, and should know sorrow only as they grieved for the sins of the world."

"For their desire to labor in bringing souls unto Christ as long as the world should stand, they were promised an eventual fullness of joy, even like unto that to which the Lord Himself has attained." *(Jesus the Christ, by James E. Talmage. Deseret Book Co. 1976. pg. 739-740.)*

Lee A. Palmer, in his book entitled, "Aaronic Priesthood Through The Centuries" explains that translated beings are "those who have lived as mortals upon the earth and who, because of their great righteousness have been changed without having to pass through death; without having their spirits separated from their physical bodies. Translated beings remain mortal; they are not immortal."

Third Nephi 28:37-38 reads, "... there must needs be a change wrought upon their bodies, or else it needs be that they must taste of death;

Therefore, that they might not taste of death there was a change wrought upon their bodies, that they might not suffer pain nor sorrow save it were for the sins of the world. *(3 Nephi 28:37-38.)*

"Translated beings are beyond the power of Satan, beyond the power of death, beyond the power of this earth. When Christ comes, they will be 'changed in the twinkling of an eye from mortality to immortality' without the separation of the spirit from the body in death."

Palmer goes on to say that, "Translated beings will never spend time in paradise, 'the world of spirits', awaiting their resurrection. The time they would have spent in paradise, if they had not been translated, is spent as ministering angels. When translated beings are 'changed in the twinkling of an eye from mortality to immortality', they will be no more as ministering angels but will be 'received into the kingdom of the Father to go no more out, but to dwell with God eternally in the heavens'."

"The Three Nephite disciples, when translated, become 'as the angels of heaven and have been ministering to men on this earth for nineteen centuries'. They will remain as such until they are quickened at the coming of Christ." *(Aaronic Priesthood Through The Centuries, by Lee A. Palmer. Deseret Book Co. 1964. pgs. 301-302.)*

Joseph F. Smith, sixth President of the Church of Jesus Christ of Latter-day Saints in speaking of "heavenly manifestations" to the Lamanites was quoted as saying, "And yet a Latter-day Saint, who knows something of the history of those people and of the promises made to them by their forefathers, hearing the same story, would conclude that perhaps one or more of the Three Nephite disciples who tarried, whose mission was to minister to the remnants of their own race, had made an appearance...and perhaps to many others, and taught them Jesus was crucified and risen from the dead, and that He was soon to come again in power and great glory to avenge them of their wrongs upon the wicked and restore them to their lands and to the knowledge of their fathers and of the Son of God."

Concerning the nature of translated beings, the Prophet Joseph Smith said, "Many have supposed that the doctrine of translation was a doctrine whereby men were taken immediately into the presence of God, and into an eternal fullness, but this is a mistaken idea. Their place of habitation is that of the terrestrial order, and a place prepared for such characters He held in reserve to be ministering angels unto many planets, and who as yet have not entered into so great a fullness as those who are resurrected from the dead....translation obtains deliverance from the tortures and sufferings of the body, but their existence will prolong as to the labors and toils of the ministry, before they can enter into so great a rest and glory. *(History of the Church 4:210. Oct. 5, 1840.)*

The Lord has given us the keys by which we are able to recognize translated beings and angels of God: "When a messenger comes saying he has a message from God, offer him your hand and request him to shake hands with you. If he be an angel he will do so, and you will feel his hand. If he be the spirit of a just man made perfect he will come in his glory; for that is the only way he can appear. Ask him to shake hands with you, but he will not move, because it is contrary to the order of heaven for a just man to deceive; but he will still deliver his message. If it be the devil as an angel of light, when you ask him to shake hands he will offer you his hand, and you will not feel anything; you may therefore detect him." *(D & C 129:4-8.)*

On the following pages, you will read historical events and personal experiences of individuals offering sincere testimony and inspirational stories which have literally changed their lives for good. In working on a project of this nature, there were some who attempted to discourage us, minimizing the importance of such information. But as you have just read, the Lord, through the Prophet Joseph Smith, (as well as many other church leaders) has stressed the importance of obtaining such valuable information. We believe that if it is found within the books of Holy Scripture, it must be of infinite worth to all Latter-day Saints. If these plain and precious truths have been preserved by prophets of God to come forth in the Latter-days, for the benefit of all of God's children, then study them we must. To say that these matters should "not be delved into" or are "too dangerous to ponder or write about" is to deny the Spirit and the scriptures. Detailed information and factual accounts and testimonies were included in the Standard Works of The Church of Jesus Christ of Latter-day Saints for the sole purpose of spiritual instruction; to encourage and assist each of us into patterning our lives in duplicity to Christ and His leading disciples. What better examples to follow than that of translated beings such as John the Beloved, Elijah, Enoch and his people, Noah, Moses, and possibly Alma the younger and Nephi, the son of Helaman...and in this volume, the Three Nephites? Of course we do not know all that has occurred, or all that was involved, but for the Savior Himself to select saints who were so righteous and worthy to be "celestially translated" is a subject to be studied above all else. For this reason, we have written and compiled this book. For your prayerful edification; to lift and motivate you to heights possibly yet unattained. Please read these pages with the same openness with which they are offered, rejoicing in the Lord and in the Gospel of Jesus Christ which is given with love to us all.

Should you, or someone you know, have a similar spiritual experience which you feel the need to bear testimony of in future accounts regarding the Three Nephites, contact the publisher at:

LDS BOOK PUBLICATIONS
Editorial Board
Box 1515
Provo, UT 84603

Chapter One

The Voyages Of Christopher Columbus

Did A Crew Member Meet The "Three Nephites"?

The 500 year commemoration of Christopher Columbus and his voyages and subsequent discovery of the Americas in the year 1492 has always been known as a blessed event and an inspirational occurrence by Latter-day Saints. There are some in modern America who downplay the importance of the Columbus voyages and discoveries, claiming America was actually discovered by some other group first. Some politically active groups attempt to revise history and our accounts of Columbus by inventing charges that he was a marauding invader; that Columbus was an intruder and invader of a supposedly tranquil people who lived in harmony with nature and each other prior to the "invasion." This is simply not true, and the facts do not justify the charges, now over 500 years old!

Left out of most modern discussion about Columbus was his true motivation for making a journey that, despite his navigational error (he thought he was discovering a new trade route to India) produced the most significant discovery in history.

Columbus was a devout Christian who saw himself as God's instrument in the fulfillment of biblical prophecy to take the Christian Gospel of redemption to new lands in every corner of the Earth. In 1 Nephi 13:12 the Prophet Nephi saw a vision of the discovery and colonizing of America saying, "And I looked and beheld a man among the Gentiles, who was separated from the seed of my brethren by the many waters; and I beheld the Spirit of God, that it came down and wrought upon the man; and he went forth upon the many waters, even unto the seed of my brethren, who were in the promised land."

Christopher Columbus was also a scholar, fluent in Latin and knowing enough Greek and Hebrew to be able to read the Bible in its original languages. Some modern scholars and history revisionists try to ascribe Columbus with wicked intentions, but a careful reading of his copied logbook and of his "Prophecies", which he wrote in the years 1501-1502 after his third voyage, shows the opposite to be true.

Many of Columbus' contemporaries opposed him. Some of the religious leaders of the time opposed him on religious grounds. Saboteurs attempted to damage the ship Pinta so it could not sail. But Columbus was supported by King Ferdinand and Queen Isabella and by what he described as the comfort and direction of God: "It was the Lord who put into my mind (I could feel His hand upon me) the fact that it would be possible to sail from here to the Indies."

"All who heard of my project rejected it with laughter, ridiculing me. There is no question that the inspiration was from the Holy Spirit, because He comforted me with rays of marvelous illumination from the Holy Scriptures..."

To those who claim Columbus pillaged the land and exploited the inhabitants he found on his voyages, reading his logbook proves otherwise. He is warmly complimentary of the beauty and gentleness he saw in those he encountered. His motives were not riches or fame, but simply to introduce those he met to their Creator and to share with them the Christian Gospel. It is true that some who followed Columbus did not share his spiritual vision, but that in no way diminishes his accomplishments under the guiding hand of the Lord.

Found in Volume 6 of The Life and Voyages of Christopher Columbus by Washington Irving, he states that Columbus "...attributed his early and irresistible inclination for the sea, and his passion for geographical studies, to an impulse from Deity, preparing him for the high decrees he was chosen to accomplish."

Upon requesting financial support from the king and queen of Spain, "he unfolded his plan with eloquence and zeal; for he felt himself, as he afterwards declared, kindled as with a fire from on high, and considered himself the chosen agent by heaven to accomplish its grand designs."

During Columbus' second voyage of discovery to America, he was sailing along the coast of what we now call Cuba, when one day he anchored off shore, near a beautiful palm grove, and Irving writes, "Here a party was sent on the shore for wood and water; and they found two living springs in the midst of the grove. While they were employed in cutting wood and filling their water casks, an archer strayed into the forest with his crossbow in search for game, but soon returned, flying with great terror, and calling loudly upon his companions for aid."

"He declared that he had not proceeded far, when he suddenly espied through an opening glade, a man in a long white dress so that at first sight he took him for a chaplain of the admiral. Two others followed in white tunics reaching to their knees, and the three were of as fair complexions as Europeans."

"Behind these appeared many more, to the number of thirty, armed with clubs and lances. They made no signs of hostility, but remained quiet, the man in the long white dress alone advancing to accost him. But he was so alarmed by their number that he fled instantly to seek the aid of his companions. The latter, however, were so daunted by the reported number of armed natives, that they had not courage to seek them nor await their coming, but hurried with all speed to the ships." *(The Life and Voyages of Christopher Columbus, by Washington Irving. Peter Fenelon Collier, New York. 1897. Volume 6, pgs. 64, 329.)*

Columbus sent two different expeditions in search of the three white men and their followers, but both expeditions returned unsuccessful. It was important to attempt to locate the "three" and their followers because no tribe of Indian inhabitants of those particular islands wore clothing, let alone, long white robes.

It is not difficult to believe that the Three Nephites could have been among the people, living with them, teaching them and fulfilling their missionary endeavors. They would have taught the inhabitants to wear clothing and they would also have been prepared to protect themselves with clubs and lances against their savage neighbors.

It is also recorded that Columbus and his sailors were looked upon by natives as visitors from heaven, and word of their appearance traveled throughout the lands. The movement of the ships was carefully watched from the shores by native inhabitants bewildered and excited by the immense size of the wooden ships and their great white billowing sails.

Chapter Two

Our Flag And The Constitution

"Were Any of the Three Nephites There?

The Committee of Three, with Franklin as chairman, was appointed by the Colonial Congress on Sept. 13, 1775, to design a flag. They met on Dec. 13, 1775, at that certain Cambridge secret home, including its host and hostess.

There they found "a stranger, or professor," who looked to be over 70 years of age, who had a curious box filled with ancient writings which he closely guarded. He knew all details of the past 100 years of American history.

George Washington, the fourth and honorary member, and Benjamin Franklin made him the 6th member of this committee. The "Stranger" then requested that their hostess be made the 7th member.

The "Stranger" also asked to be the first speaker. He then submitted a drawing of this flag. It was accepted at once and the "Stranger" disappeared.

This flag was made. George Washington personally hoisted it on Jan. 1, 1776, over his camp and army, on a specially prepared pole, and both his and the English army at a distance, saluted it with 13 cheers and 13 guns. It is called the "Grand Union", also the Cambridge flag, and has the Union Jack in place of the stars.

The "Stranger" stated that in order to unite the 13 colonies in their separation from their mother country, the Union Jack was necessary to begin with, and later on could be changed. This Union Jack was replaced June 14, 1777, with a blue field having 13 stars in a circle, which became our second national flag, and was designed by Elizabeth (Betsy) Ross.

Now it was apparently this same "Stranger" who again appeared at Philadelphia on July 4, 1776. Speaker after speaker had failed to rally the delegates (who feared for their lives) to sign the prepared Declaration of Independence. The old bellman finally said, "No, they never will sign it."

When one o'clock came, a penetrating voice rang out, ringing with holy zeal. The debating stopped and everyone listened. It was not the voice of mortal man — for it stirred their inner souls. His divine counsel and commanding voice strengthened their faith and gave them courage to back it up. The speaker ended with these words: "God has given America to be free."

The immediate signing of the document began, and the prepared bell of liberty, at 2 p.m. sent their decree around the world. A child, a nation, destined for God's greatest blessings, was born — their Declaration of Liberty was signed — but the "Stranger" was gone. *(America's Thirteen Colonial States.)*

Chapter Three

Hill Cumorah Visit

George Q. Cannon

I have had my thoughts attracted, in consequence of a visit which Brother Brigham, Jr., and myself made to the Hill Cumorah about three weeks ago, to the Three Nephites who have been upon this land, and I have been greatly comforted at reading the promises of God concerning their labors and the work that should be accomplished by them among the Gentiles and among the Jews, also before the coming of the Lord Jesus. I doubt not that they are laboring today in the great cause on the earth. There are agencies laboring for the accomplishment of the purposes of God and for the fulfillment of the predictions of the holy Prophets, of which we have but little conception at the present time. We are engrossed in our own labors. You in Cache Valley have your thoughts centered on the labors that devolve upon you. We in Salt Lake and elsewhere have ours upon the work that immediately attracts our attention; and while we, or all amongst us who are faithful, shall no doubt be instrumental in the hands of God, in bringing to pass His purposes and accomplishing the work He has predicted in connection with the Ten Tribes, the Lamanites, the Jews, and the Gentile nations, we need not think that these things depend upon us alone. There are powers engaged in preparing the earth for the events that await it and fulfilling all the great predictions concerning it, which we know nothing of, and we need not think that it depends upon us Latter-day Saints alone, and that we are the only agents in the hands of God in bringing these things to pass. The powers of heaven are engaged with us in this work. *(Journal of Discourses, Vol. 16:120.)*

Chapter Four

Indian Chiefs And The President

Chief Tabiona

In the year 1873 Bishop A.K. Thurber and George W. Bean were authorized to appoint a small company to explore Rabbit Valley and visit and make treaty with the Indians inhabiting that region. William Robertson and William Jex were appointed to serve in this capacity with Bishop Thurber and Mr. Bean. They left in June of that year to fill their appointment, being equipped with riding horses and pack animals. They had with them as their guide and interpreter an Indian chief by the name of Tabiona. They went by way of Nephi, Warm Creek through Salina, and thence to Glenwood. From here they made their way through King's Meadows and on to Fish Lake. At the latter point they found a band of Indians with Poganeab as their chief, better known, perhaps, as "Fish Lake Chief."

After supper on the evening of the first day they had a long talk with the Indians. Both Thurber and

Bean understood the Indian language and they acted as interpreters. The Indians were told briefly the history of their forefathers as contained in the Book of Mormon, and were presented with a volume of this record. They were intensely interested and related many of the happenings of their tribe. Chief Tabiona, the Indian guide, related a circumstance that happened when he and other Indian chiefs went to Washington, D.C., to talk with the "Big Chief." He said that while they were talking to the President of the United States and some of the officials, that they, the Indians, saw three persons of fine appearance, dressed in white robes, enter the room. The "white men" did not see them, but the Indians saw them and were convinced that the heavenly messengers were friends of the Indians.

This circumstance made a great impression on the Indians, and led them to believe that the "Great Chief" was their friend and was looking after their interests. Mr. Jex and the other visitors surmised that these three personages were the Three Nephites spoken of in the Book of Mormon, who were to remain on earth until the second advent of the Savior.

The journey continued to the lower end of Rabbit Valley, and explorations were made of the mountains and district to the south. Having completed the work assigned them, the party started on the homeward journey, going by way of the east fork of the

Sevier River. It had been arranged to have all the settlers of Grass Valley district, as well as the Indians in the vicinity, meet in a "Peace Talk" at Cedar Grove.

A large number of Indians gathered from the surrounding country. To them were distributed gifts, and explanation was made of the friendly attitude of the white man and his purpose in making settlements in the country. From all appearances a good impression was made on the Indians and the exploring party felt that it had accomplished its mission. Return was made by way of San Pete County and Thistle Valley. Here Chief Tabiona met his squaw awaiting his return. *(William Jex, Pioneer and Patriarch. Spanish Fork Press. 1920. pgs. 46-50.)*

Chapter Five

Bread, Buttermilk and Brigham Young

H.B. Campbell

One morning in the summer of 1865, father had gone to work and mother was about her household duties. About ten o'clock a man appeared at the door. He was dressed in a linen suit, a white shirt and a straw hat. He had a long, white beard. She answered the door and he asked for something to eat. At first she was startled as she gazed upon him. Her fear subsided and she invited him in. She wondered why a person like he should come to such a humble home, for the house was just a one-room with a lean-to and cellar, with a little porch at one side.

She told him that all she had in the house was some bread and buttermilk, to which he replied, "These are the very things I like best." While mother was preparing the food she placed a white cover on the table, she noticed he was darning a little rent in his coat sleeve. She bid him set up and he ate heartily of the bread and buttermilk. As he arose to depart, he thanked her and blessed her with this promise: "That she would never see the day that she would be without bread in the house." On departing, he asked where a certain man lived. As he left she cleared the table and shook the cloth and he had vanished from view. Upon inquiry of the neighbors, no man had been seen of that description.

A short time after this happened, Brigham Young came through Providence to whom she related the incident, and he told her it was one of the Three Nephites. The blessing surely came true, because she was never without bread, and for 50 years furnished the bread for the sacrament meeting in the Providence Ward. *(Heart Throbs of the West, by Kate B. Carter. Daughters of Utah Pioneers. 1941. Vol. 3, pg. 353.)*

Chapter Six

Strangers To Teach Us

Brigham Young

Brigham Young, who recognized the ministry of the Nephites, said in 1859:

"Pretty soon you will see Temples reared up, and the sons of Jacob will enter into the Temples of the lord. ...there will be strangers in your midst walking with you, talking with you; they will enter your houses and eat and drink with you; go to meeting with you, and begin to open your minds, as the Saviour did the two disciples who walked out in the country in the days of old. ...They will expound the Scriptures to you, and open your minds, and teach you the time of Salvation; they will use the keys of the holy Priesthood, and unlock the door of Knowledge, to let you look into the place of truth. You will exclaim. That is all plain: Why did I not understand it before? And you will begin to feel your hearts burn within you as they walk and talk with you."

(Brigham Young, "Strangers to Appear," Journal of

Discourses, Vol. 6, 1858, pp. 194-5. Quoted as a reference to the Nephites by Robert W. Smith and Elisabeth A. Smith, in Scriptural and Secular Prophecies Pertaining to the Last Days. Salt Lake City: Privately Published, 1943, pp. 44-45.)

Although Brigham Young does not mention the Nephites specifically here, it is generally considered by scriptural scholars that the Three Nephites were meant in this passage.

Chapter Seven

A Translated Being Prescribes

Elizabeth J. Barney and
J. Orson Barney

My father's name was William Cooke Prows and my mother's name was Louisa M. R. James. I was born in Kanosh, Millard County, Utah, on the 17th of June, 1877. I was the 5th child of a family of eight of my father's second wife. In the spring of 1893, my father, with my mother and children and one of the first wife's grandchildren, were going from Mesa, Arizona, to Juarez, Mexico, for the purpose of establishing a home. We had lived in Mesa but a few months prior to this. In the company were J. Orson Barney (who later became my husband), Isaac Miller, Mrs. Osborne Colley and family, and the members of the family as before mentioned. We had passed through El Paso, Texas, and had traveled several days out into the desert. There were three wagons and one buggy in this caravan. The trip from Mesa to Mexico took about a month. After several days journey from Tucson, my mother became very sick which continued to increase in intensity as time went on. She had hemorrhage after hemorrhage. Her hands had been cold and blue for two days. It was then my father desired to get out of the sand belt into a country where gravel could be located, for the purpose, as he later stated, to find a suitable place to bury mother, as he feared that she would pass on any minute, and as he went about that morning tears were seen in his eyes, but he never revealed why he felt sorrowful. On this certain day, he started very early in the morning in order to make as much distance as possible, but, after travelling a few hours, my mother stated that she could not stand the jarring any longer, in her weakened and desperately sick condition. So camp was made and preparations were started for making breakfast. While thus preparing things for breakfast, a man suddenly appeared in camp not more than ten or twenty feet away and upon coming up he stated: "Good morning." To which my father answered: "Good morning." The stranger said: "How are you?" To which my father replied: "I have a mighty sick wife." The stranger enquired: "Where is she?" Father said: "She is over here in the wagon," at the same time both of them started toward the wagon, which upon reaching, father raised the wagon cover and both looked in, father introducing the stranger with: "Eliza, here is a man who has come to see you." The stranger extended his hand and placed it on her forehead and gently rubbed her head, saying: "How are you feeling, sister?" To which my mother replied: "I sure don't feel very good." While at the wagon, they all three had a short conversation. I was standing on the wagon wheel all this time, paying careful attention to all that was said and done. After talking but a few minutes, he said: "Come out here and I will show you something to give your wife and she will be all right and you can be on your way within an hour." A short scrubby tree with some green berries on it was near, which the stranger called "Juniper Berries." After taking a few of these he went a short distance and told father to gather the leaves from a small shrub growing in the desert at this particular place but which was not noticed at other places along the road. He told my father to, "take some of the Juniper berries and the leaves from the bush," he showed him, "and mix them together, steep them and give them to your wife and you can be on your way within an hour." After making this statement the stranger said: "I must be going."

My father replied: "Man, you must stay and have breakfast with us. There will be many miles before you can get a drink of water or a bite to eat. I have been over this road many times and know it." Father insisted that he stay and have breakfast but he raised his cap and said: "I must be on my way. Your wife will be all right," and at saying this he smiled and said "Good-day." At the time he placed his hand upon my mother's forehead she felt like a new person, the touch of his hand was soothing and healing. One of the children at the breakfast fire did something which drew our attention to them and upon looking up, the stranger had suddenly vanished and father said: "Where did he go?" They all walked out to see if he could be seen but no trace of him was visible. My father exclaimed: "Gracious! Golly! where could that man have gone?" Nothing but the desert road was before them and small scrubby desert growth extended all around as far as the eye could se. The tea was made and given to my mother who soon revived. She ate breakfast and helped to prepare supper that evening for the group, assisted by me.

The stranger was of medium size, dressed in a grayish blue suit, and wore a grayish beard, some three or four inches long. He looked very intelligent and clean cut. His voice was soft and mild and his eyes penetrating but beautiful to behold. There was something about his personality that caused us to look at him with intent and earnestness.

Upon arriving in Mexico, we rented a lot with a small house on it from a Brother Thompson whose wife and two sons had been killed by the Indians but a short time before. My father put in a garden but died within two months after arriving, but before passing he said to my mother one day: "Eliza, I want you to go back to Utah and see that my father is sealed to my mother and their children sealed to their parents," for they had all been sealed to President Brigham Young.

This sealing was attended to by President Lorenzo Snow. By signing our names to this narrative, we attest its absolute truthfulness:

Elizabeth J. Barney
J. Orson Barney
Witnessed by - William N. Stevens

(Assorted Gems of Priceless Value, by N.B. Lundwall. 1944. pgs. 28-30.)

Chapter Eight

Three Nephites Taught Them

Melvin J. Ballard

Through the modern educational advancement of these people our elders can proselyte among these native sons of America and deliver the message of the Book of Mormon and the gospel of Jesus Christ. The Indians can read and understand it; years ago they could not. With no written language it would have been difficult to explain the principles of the gospel, without a thorough knowledge of the Indian tongues.

When Elder Melvin J. Ballard visited the Ft. Peck and Blackfoot reservations he said he met many who knew him as soon as they saw him and asked for the "Book" which he was to bring them. They said they had seen him in dreams, bringing to them a "Book." When he handed them the Book of Mormon they adopted it gladly, and could read and understand it. He declared that it was his belief that one of the "Three Nephites" had been laboring among them for years teaching them the gospel and preparing them for our missionaries when they should come.

Branches of the Church have been organized among the Indians in various states, and some of the Indians have been ordained to the Aaronic and some to the Melchizedek Priesthood. *(Improvement Era, Vol. 27: 420. Annie M. Holdaway.)*

Chapter Nine

Missionary Records Located

Keith A. Winder

I have strong reason to believe that I had an experience with one of the Three Nephites while serving a Spanish speaking mission in the California Fresno Mission in the summer of 1988. I have included a description of the events surrounding the encounter and I am willing to provide any other details I may have left out.

I hope you find the experience uplifting. I have not shared this experience with many people, only to those who I can trust not to make light of it, because I hold it as a sacred experience. I testify that what I have written is true. Nothing is added to "spice up" the story, but it is described in the way it happened. I have also included my personal feelings during the experience.

I prefer to remain anonymous, but if it is required, I may include my name in the experience.

Thank you for your time spent reading this experience. I hope it may be used to uplift and inspire others.

It happened in the first area I served on my mission, Corcoron, California. Corcoron is a small town in the San Joaquin Valley which is surrounded by acres and acres of cotton plantations. When I served there in the summer of 1988, the small branch of the church met in the local YMCA each Sunday for church meetings. The whole town had a total of no more than three stoplights, so it was one of those towns where practically everyone knew who everyone else was.

We lived behind a member's home, the Adamson family, in a small one room studio apartment. Living so close to a member family was nice as we socialized with the family quite often. One Monday evening after returning to our apartment for supper, my companion and I saw Brother and Sister Adamson in their driveway, ready to leave somewhere, and we stopped to chat with them for a few minutes. I thoughtlessly set our area book on top of their minivan and, upon ending our conversation, left it on the car's roof. We then went back to our apartment to eat and they took off in their car, along with our area book still on the roof.

The next morning, upon searching the apartment for our precious area book, to our dismay, we could not find it. Those of you who know how important an area book is to a missionary can relate to the despair I felt at the time, realizing that over five years of investigator records were lost. Additionally, I had left my weekly planner in the area book, so we didn't know which appointments were scheduled for that week.

That week, I fasted and prayed very earnestly that we could be able to find our area book. I am an absent-minded person by nature and I knew that I had misplaced it somewhere, but I could not imagine how I could have lost it in a one room studio apartment. More than once I had left my things at members' homes, but none of the members said that I left the area book in their home.

Anyway, the week went on and we did the best we could to remember all of the addresses and appointments of our investigators. Fortunately, we remembered most of them.

Four days passed since we had seen the area book and I was beginning to accept the fact that five years of missionary records were lost and that I would be responsible for those people who would have accepted the gospel had I not lost the area book. However, I did not give up hope. Every morning and night I prayed that somehow we would find the area book. Then, I witnessed a miracle that I have never forgotten. It was a very simple miracle, but it has left a lasting impression upon my mind that the Lord does watch over his missionaries, even in their absentmindedness.

It was Friday at around 6:30 p.m. and we were just getting out of our car to visit a part member family (this was one of the appointments we were able to remember). As we walked to the door, a man drove up in a white car and got out and walked directly up to my companion and I. In his hand was our long lost area book, a bit dusty and beaten up, but still containing all of the information it had before. The man was about six feet tall, had white curly hair and must have weighed about 195 pounds. He was clean shaven and had a smile on his face as he held out the area book to me and asked, "Does this belong to you?"

Overwhelmed, I looked at the book and exclaimed, "Yes! Where did you find it?"

"I was driving along the highway a few miles north of here and saw it on the side of the road in a ditch," said the stranger.

"How did you find us then?" I asked, never having seen the man or his car in the small town.

He quickly explained that he looked at my blue planner in the book and found the address where we would be at 6:30 on Friday.

Still in disbelief, I shook his hand and thanked him and thumbed through the book to make sure it was real and that I wasn't just hallucinating. Meanwhile, the man quietly left and drove off before I had a chance to ask his name or to inquire as to where he lived or if he were interested in hearing more about the church.

I related this experience to the members of the Corcoron branch, but none of them had ever seen the man or the car the way I described them. (In such a small town, believe it or not, even the cars are known). Others stated that one of the Three Nephites had retrieved my area book. I denied this possibility at first, but in the five months I served in tiny Corcoron, California, I never saw the man or his car again, nor did any of the members to my knowledge.

The Lord does watch over His missionaries and He does hear their prayers. He heard mine and He answered it. The Three Nephites have an ongoing mission on this earth to help in the missionary efforts. I know they are on the earth today. I cannot say that I have a testimony that I met one of the Three Nephites, but I can say that I hold it as a strong possibility because of the circumstances present. The man who gave me my area book was an anonymous servant in this case. He left no name and asked for no reward. Whoever he was, he was the Lord's instrument in answering a prayer of an earnest missionary.
(Submitted by Elder Keith A. Winder, October 26, 1992.)

Chapter Ten

Enoch's Temples

Franklin D. Richards

This view of the subject brings me to think and to speak a word in reference to the Three Nephites. They wanted to tarry until Jesus came, and that they might,He took them into the heavens and endowed them with the power of translation, probably in one of Enoch's temples, and brought them back to the earth. Thus they received power to live until the coming of the Son of Man. I believe He took them to Enoch's city and gave them their endowments there. I expect that in the city of Enoch there are temples; and when Enoch and his people come back, they will come back with their city, their temples, blessings and powers. The north country will yield up its multitude, with the Apostle John, who is looking after them. They also will come to Zion and receive their crowns at the hands of their brethren of Ephraim. There will also be nations here on the earth that have not received the Gospel, but who will receive it, and thus the work of God will

go on in all its phases, for the living and for the dead.
(Journal of Discourses, Vol. 25, pgs. 236-237, Logan Tabernacle, May 17, 1884.)

Chapter Eleven

Albert, The Bright Stone

This is about Albert, an Indian boy, the adopted son of Jacob Hamblin, the great pioneer and Indian interpreter. In the year 1850, Hamblin and his family with other Saints settled in Tooele Valley which was at that time inhabited by a band of Indians led by a chief called Old Big Foot. Old Big Foot was a bad Indian and he and his followers caused the white settlers a great deal of trouble by their depredations, which, despite the efforts of the people of Salt Lake and Tooele to quell them, continued to last about three years.

Finally Hamblin, who was then lieutenant, asked that a company be given him with which to make a raid on the Indians; he succeeded finally, not in killing them, but in effecting a peace with them. During this raid against them he had become convinced by the manifestations of the Holy Spirit in many instances that his calling was not to fight and kill the Indians, but it was to be a messenger of love and peace to them, and by this same spirit it was also made manifest to him that if he would not thirst for their blood, he should never fall by their hands. This precious promise of the Almighty through His spirit to Hamblin was a source of great strength and assurance to him in after years, and enabled him while among the Indians to pass through scenes unmoved which caused some of the bravest of other men to tremble.

Soon after his return from trailing after Old Big Foot he dreamed that he was on a friendly visit to the Indians they had been so long trying to destroy, and while walking and talking with them he picked up a stone. This on being touched, diffused a bright phosphorescent light, and as he handled it, the light stuck to his fingers, and as he tried to brush it away it continued to spread over him.

This dream made a great impression upon him and was repeated to him for three successive nights. At the third repetition of it he arose from his bed, saddled his horse and taking his gun and blankets went alone into the Indian country. He entered the valley where their lodges had stood when he was there before but saw no Indians, but a smoke curled up near the center of the valley. He directed his way to it and found there sitting on a rock nearby a little Indian boy about ten years old, who was crying bitterly. The spirit said to Hamblin as he addressed the boy, "This is the bright stone you saw in your dream; take the lad home with you." He asked the boy the cause of his grief; he replied by pointing to an old lodge nearby where an Indian woman, the boy's mother, lay dying. The other Indians, according to their custom at such times, had gone away and left her to die alone. He asked the boy if he would like to go home with him; he replied that he would, but added, "I want you to come and heal my mother first." Hamblin went with the boy to where his mother lay and administered to her by laying hands upon her and she soon after sat up and conversed with him. Though he knew very little of their language, yet by the gift of tongues he was enabled to understand them and to make himself understood.

They told him they had known all day that he would come to them, and the boy afterwards said, when Hamblin asked him why he was so willing to go with him, the first white man he had ever seen and a stranger, that "three men" having white hair and beards came and told him of his (Hamblin's) visit and advised him to go home with the white man when he came.

The fire had been built to attract the expected visitor's attention to the spot.

Though the mother had readily given her consent when Hamblin first asked for the boy to go with him, yet when about to depart and the little fellow picked up his bows and arrows, she set up such a wail that Hamblin's heart was touched and he told the boy to go back and remain with her; but the lad refused to do so and followed his new guardian. That night, the mother, still anxious about her son, came to the camp and told Hamblin she was willing for him to take her boy, for she believed he was a good man, but exacted the promise from him that he would always be a father to him and own him for a son. Hamblin gave the promise and was always faithful to the trust.

The boy Albert was very much attached to his adopted father who was his only confidant and friend, and he was an obedient and faithful son to him. As he grew older, the care of his father's flocks was given him and they increased rapidly while under his management.

He manifested a great love for the gospel and its teachings, had many dreams and visions but had also many trials and temptations. One day after having made some remark about his mission on the earth, he was questioned by his father when he confessed to him that he had many times met with and received counsel from his "three friends" as he called them; he had been reticent about speaking of it to his father for fear of his displeasure, but when he found he was to receive only encouragement from him, his pleasure knew no bounds. He seemed imbued with the idea that he had a mission to perform among his race in the spirit world; he was ordained to the offices of the lower priesthood and when he had arrived at the age of manhood, he told his father one day that the time had come for him to receive his endowments, for he was soon to go on his mission, and it was necessary that he should receive his blessings first. For some cause it was not convenient for him to go in the House of the Lord at that time; when his father told him he would have to wait awhile, he said "Then I shall have to suffer." Soon after he was stricken with erysipelas in his eyes and face and was not healed until his father started with him from Santa Clara, where he then lived, for Salt Lake City, where he received his endowments.

In 1863, twelve years from the time when Albert picked up his bows and arrows and left his Indian haunts for the home of his white friends, as Hamblin was leaving home on a mission to the Moquis Indians, he approached him and said, "Father, I shall be on my mission before you get back again." His father asked him what he meant and he said, "My time has come to

go and I shall be dead and buried before your return."
When Hamblin returned at the expiration of two
months, he found Albert's place vacant; he has passed
away as he had, the morning of his father's departure,
predicted. *(Juvenile Instructor, Vol. 22:332.)*

Chapter Twelve

A *Mysterious* Visitor

Anne Rencher Price

James Rencher's description of an unusual experience follows:

"My hobby was fine horses and I always drove a fiery spirited team of which I was very proud. I freighted a great deal over Utah and Nevada, but I made it a rule never to ask strangers to ride with me — my horses didn't like them and neither did I. One day in the early spring, while I was on my way from St. George to the ranch at Grass Valley, a man suddenly appeared beside the road. My horses didn't notice him or seem to be frightened at all, which was unusual, so I stopped and asked the stranger to ride with me, a thing I had never done before. He readily accepted and climbed into the seat beside me. We immediately began to chat about the weather, etc., and then our conversation drifted to politics, religion, books, and people, and no matter what subject came up, I was amazed at the wealth of knowledge the stranger displayed. He conversed intelligently on everything and he answered a lot of questions for me that I had pondered over a great deal. As we rode along I got out my lunch and asked the stranger to have a sandwich with me, but he declined, saying he wasn't hungry. Then as we drove through the little town of Pine Valley, no one saw this man sitting beside me although different ones saw me drive through."

"We traveled together several hours and chatted amiably all the while until along about sundown the stranger asked me how far it was to the next town and I told him it was nine miles, and as it was getting late and quite cold, I invited him to come up and spend the night with me. Again he graciously refused, simply saying he had work to do. But I insisted that it was far too late for him to make the next town before night and I assured him I would enjoy having a longer visit with him, but he quietly declined, saying: "My friend, I have other work to do."

"As he got out of the wagon a flock of quail flew up out of the brush, frightening my horses, and my attention was diverted to them for a minute, and as I turned to look for my 'friend' he was nowhere in sight."

Uncle Jim believed, from the unusual knowledge the stranger displayed and the wealth of information he gave, and also the fact that he refused to stay overnight with him, that he had had the privilege of seeing one of the Three Nephites. *(Heart Throbs of the West, by Kate B. Carter. Daughter of Utah Pioneers. 1941. Vol. 3, pg. 351.)*

Chapter Thirteen

Pulled From The River

Louise S. Richards

We lived on South Second between Fourth and Fifth East, and when my brothers were young they went straight down Second South to the Jordan River to fish. One day, mother said she didn't want to give her consent, but they coaxed a little, and she finally relented and she put up a lunch in a basket that had a handle over it but had no cover, and off they went. After a while mother got kind of restless. She felt worried, and she went in her little bedroom and prayed. Earlier than she thought they'd be home, my brother came back. He was an impulsive boy and he liked to tease, but he got up close to mother.

The young man that he'd gone fishing with came along the street just then and said to George, "Well, how do you feel after your drowning?" My father and mother looked at him and my mother said, "What do you mean? So then of course George told us what had happened.

When they got down to the Jordan the young man told him to take the lunch and put it on the ground a little way along the bank, and then catch some minnies, so George ran as fast as he could along the bank. The ground was perfectly level. There wasn't any hill or any clumps of bushes around, but suddenly there was an old man in front of him who said, "Look out, sonny." But being a boy, George went right on doing what he was doing and ran right out into the river, still holding the basket. The old man just reached out and grabbed him and pulled him out. Mother had always taught us to respect our elders and be polite to them, and George was quite a polite boy, so he turned around to thank the old man, and he had disappeared. There wasn't any hill or anything, but he had vanished. George said it was one of the Three Nephites, and mother and father thought so, too. I think it was too.

(The Three Nephites, by Hector Haight Lee. The University of New Mexico. 1949. pgs. 151-152.)

Chapter Fourteen

No Footprints

Clarissa Young (Spencer)

During a winter in the early 70's my father, president Brigham Young, was planning to take me to Provo to attend Brother Karl G. Maeser's school. I am not going to tell of the real excitement I got out of the fact I was going on a long trip with Father and the planning by Mother, bless her memory, of my dresses and a coat, etc., to see me through school for the winter. And such pretty dresses they were for those days -- a lovely magenta delaine with a broad border braided in black silk braid and a black alpaca dress trimmed with narrow black ribbon velvet. My coat was made of heavy brown woolen material with shoulder cape which was scalloped and bound with brown silk braid with a cap to match of brown velveteen.

We left Salt Lake early one crisp morning, stopping at one of the settlements on the way for lunch. All the people we met seemed happy to have Father stop long enough for lunch and to feed the horses and when we left gave us a great sendoff. That same night we reached Provo where Aunt Eliza gave us a great welcome and a lovely supper, after which we sat in the parlor, talked awhile and relaxed after our day's journey, and then Father and Aunt Eliza called everybody who was in the house to come to the parlor for evening prayers. This was always done. I never left Father's side for a moment, (possibly I was a tiny bit homesick for my mother), until time for bed, then with a good night kiss, I followed Aunt Eliza upstairs. She put me in her bed, after saying my prayers tucked me in just as Mother always did, and I was too tired to be homesick for long. A feeling of drowsiness soon came over me after sinking down in that lovely feather bed with the lamp turned low and Aunt Eliza quietly leaving the room. Then oblivion.

Aunt Eliza's home in Provo stood on the northeast corner of one of the main streets. The front of the house faced east. Just opposite, across the street, stood Bishop Smoot's house. Just across the street on the north side stood the tabernacle as it is today. Aunt Eliza's lot was surrounded by a picket fence and a path led from the front door to the main street on the east. On the north side was a porch possibly fifteen feet long in front of the dining room window and door. This room was where we usually sat, as the parlor on the northeast corner of the house was heated and opened only when we had company.

The front hall opened into the dining room and in this hall was the broad staircase which went to the upper floor. This particular winter was very cold with a great deal of snow on the ground. The north door in the dining room we always kept locked and used only the front door on the east. The purpose of this was to get the full benefit of the fire in the stove in the dining room and to keep out as much cold as possible. This is where we studied and practically lived. When I say we I mean Aunt Eliza, Johnnie Walton, a young man from Alpine who worked for his board, and went to Brother Maeser's school, and myself.

This day it had been snowing heavily for several hours, but it had cleared up and the sun was shining when I returned from school. I had to break a path from the east gate to the door through six or seven inches of snow. Johnny had remained at school this particular day and consequently no path had been swept when I returned. It must have been along about four-thirty, for I remember the sun shining through the trees, making the fence, where the snow had piled up, look like it was covered with diamonds.

Aunt Eliza and I were sitting by a fire when a gentle knock came on the north door. We were surprised, as no one ever came to that door. Aunt Eliza motioned me to answer the knock and I got up, feeling perfectly safe as our big watch dog, Rover, lay on the floor beside me. I unlocked the door and opened it and there stood a rather tall man, very pale, wearing a straw hat, blue jacket and spotless blue overalls. "Will you give me something to eat?" he asked. I turned to Aunt Eliza and repeated his question, as he had spoken in a low voice. She invited him to come in and sit down, which he did, placing his hat on the wide window sill. I laid the cloth and we set out a lunch of cold meat, apple sauce, good homemade bread and butter and a pitcher of milk. As the man came to the chair placed for him, we went to the other side of the room. Aunt Eliza to her knitting and I to my books. Old Rover raised his head, looked at the stranger peacefully and then dozed off again. This was something unusual for Rover to do for as a rule he was not friendly to strangers.

After a while the man arose and thanking us in the same subdued voice, picked up his hat and departed, quietly, closing the door behind him. There was something so unusual about the man that I jumped up and ran to the window to have a peek at him. As I passed the table I glanced down and remember distinctly saying breathlessly, "Aunt Eliza, he hasn't eaten anything at all." The food was untouched, aside from a small piece of broken bread. We hurriedly opened the door. The man was nowhere in sight and neither was there a sign of footprints in the newly fallen snow on the porch, on the path leading to the gate or around the house. I ran to the front gate to see if I could see him on the street but he had completely disappeared.

We came back into the house wondering who he was, where he had come from and where he had gone. He was dressed immaculately and his face, with the serene peaceful expression, will remain with me always. Later we made inquiries of our neighbors but none of them had seen or heard of him. Time went on but no explanation developed.

When Father returned, Aunt Eliza related our experience with the stranger and asked, "President Young, what do you think it means?" Father sat for some time twirling his thumbs as was his habit while thinking seriously. I was standing beside him. With his arm around me, waiting anxiously for his reply. As he drew me closer to him, he said very seriously and very quietly, "I believe this house has been visited by one of the Three Nephites." He paused a moment and then said, "We will all kneel and have our evening prayers."

Now just a few more lines to say that I am not trying to convince my readers of the truth of this experience which came to me when I was a child, but had I doubted the correctness of my memory, an incident occurred just a few months ago that has firmly convinced me of the fact that I have neither forgotten nor exaggerated the incident set down in the foregoing statement.

In June of this year, 1930, the telephone operator in the apartment where I live called me to say that there was a gentleman in the lobby to see me.

When I went down I immediately recognized, although I had not seen him for fifty years, John Walton, the boy who was living in Aunt Eliza's home the winter the above events took place. We had a very interesting visit talking over old times in Provo, and as he was leaving he asked me if I remembered the visit of the strange personage while we were living in Aunt Eliza's home in Provo. When I replied that I remembered it very distinctly, he asked me to repeat it to him just as I remembered it and as I have told it here. He told me he had related it to his family many times and it was a great satisfaction to me to know that I had neither added to nor taken away from his recollection of a most interesting occurrence of so many, many years ago.

A picture will always remain in my memory of that peaceful home in Provo; the great big comfortable house, the kindness and thoughtfulness of Aunt Eliza, the unbroken paths of snow surrounding the home on the day of the eventful visit of the stranger and the beautiful influence which I took with me when my dear father terminated my unusual visit. *(Improvement Era 34:232.)*

Chapter Fifteen

Panguitch Story

There was a time when such a succession of crop failures and other economic calamities visited the people of Utah that they despaired of finding succor by natural means. Being a pious people, they placed the whole of their faith in God and prayed for aid.

One Sunday afternoon the inhabitants of the little village of Panguitch had gathered for the regular sacrament meeting. Although the economic trouble was not the primary object of discussion, the problem was uppermost in the minds of all. Near the close of the meeting a dignified, elderly gentleman clothed entirely in white entered and asked permission to speak. Not doubting that he bore a message from a recognized church authority, the congregation immediately gave him attention.

The old man outlined the economic situation perfectly and counseled the people to prepare for a period of prosperity to be followed by a greater depression. He warned of the fallacy of placing money high in human estimation and, with an admonition to live clean lives and follow the church precepts, he turned and left the assembly. An official of the church followed him outside only to find that he had disappeared. Upon inquiry it was discovered that the old man had never been seen in that country before, nor did he bring a message from the central authority of the church.

Similar old men appeared at the same hour and day in the villages of Nephi and Heber City. Each had asked permission to speak at the sacrament meetings, and each had delivered the same message. *(Anonymous manuscript entitled "The Nephites" from WPA Writers' Project.)*

Chapter Sixteen

Her Child Was Healed

Matilda Y. S. Staker

In the year 1859, Thomas and Matilda Stolworthy were called from Parowan to Salt Lake City by Brigham Young. Their only child, a little girl, lay sick with a high fever — no doctor, no one to help but a kind neighbor. The mother felt as though she could not give her up, so falling on her knees, she poured out her heart and asked help from her Heavenly Father.

While she was still kneeling by the cradle, she felt a breeze come through the house, and she turned towards the door to see who had come in, and there stood a stranger in the room. He had a long white beard and wore a suit of light clothes. He had such a kind yet firm face and seemed to bring peace into the room as soon as he entered it. As Grandmother gazed upon his face, she asked him to have a chair, and was very astonished to hear him say, "No, I just came to see your sick child." Then turning to the baby he laid his hands on her head and murmured some words that they could not understand. Turning to Grandmother, he said: "Sister Stolworthy, you have had great sorrow and trouble, but you have been true and faithful through it all. God will bless you, and your little girl will grow to womanhood and raise a family of ten children, and I promise you that you will yet raise a family to manhood and womanhood." He then went to the door and went out, closing it behind him. As grandmother turned to the baby, she saw the child was sleeping.

The two women hurried to the door to ask the man who he was, but there was no one in sight. They followed his footsteps to the gate, but there they vanished. They inquired of the neighbors but no one had seen the stranger around. Grandmother always felt as though he was one of the Three Nephites that was left here on earth, as his promises were fulfilled to the letter, as Elizabeth is still alive and she had ten living children. *(Heart Throbs of the West, by Kate B. Carter. Daughters of Utah Pioneers. 1941. Vol. 3, pg. 349.)*

Chapter Seventeen

The Prophet Joseph Identifies The Stranger

William R. Sloan

"It was a cold night in the latter part of November, and in the home of William Huntington the family gathered around the big fire place in the spacious kitchen. After the evening meal, when all the evening work was done, it was the habit of this family to get their instruments of music and sit around the blazing logs and play the old fashioned tunes and hymns, also tunes of more cheerful air, although they did not dance."

"Grandfather Huntington played the bass viol, his daughter Zina the cello, William, the cornet, and Dimick, the drum. There were five sons and two daughters, the oldest daughter, Presenda, being married, lived some distance from them. It was a happy New England family and they lived the clean, pure life of the Puritan stock. After the music ceased a hush fell on the group and a knock was heard on the door and as it opened a strange old gentleman of medium weight, dressed in old fashioned clothes and carrying a bundle on his arm, appeared and stepped into the room and said: 'I usually bend my steps to some sequestered vale. May I find lodging here tonight?"

"With cordial welcome he was invited in and given a place by the fire, in an old easy farm chair, and mother Huntington asked if he would like some supper and modestly he said he would. Then a good New England meal was spread before him, with milk, honey, maple syrup, cold meat, delicious home-made bread and butter. He partook of a light supper while the family spoke in soft tones. It was the custom to read a portion of the scriptures before going to bed. He again joined the circle, and father Huntington began to read from the Holy Bible, a portion of the New Testament, to which they all listened attentively. Grandmother Huntington made some comment on the fact that they would like to hear the Gospel in its fullness as explained and taught by the Saviour. The stranger immediately took up the subject and began explaining the scriptures and quoting the sayings of the Saviour in what seemed to them a new light and greater beauty than they had ever thought of before. They sat in rapt attention listening to every word. Both father and mother Huntington agreed with his explanations while the boys exchanged glances of admiration and the daughter Zina was spellbound and sat and gazed upon the stranger with admiration and reverence. After one hour spent in conversation upon this sacred subject, father Huntington had prayers, mother Huntington prepared a comfortable resting place for the stranger and he bid them good night, the boys going upstairs, father and mother Huntington to their bed room which led from the kitchen, and Zina in her little bed heard her parents talking in low tones about the wonderful stranger and discuss the things he said. The stranger had filled them with awe and reverence, such as they had never felt before. In the morning every one was astir bright and early as is usual on a farm when so much work has to be done, both outside and in.

"The stranger sat placidly watching the remarkable family with whom he took breakfast. The family invited him to stay but he said he had other places to visit and he left them standing in a group as he closed the door softly. When father Huntington saw the stranger depart, he sent Dimick after him to tell him to come again. He immediately opened the door and they all looked out to see and call the stranger back but he was no where to be seen. When looking on the door step where the snow had fallen the night before, no trace of a footstep could be seen and the boys running from all directions said that he had vanished and could not be found. Father Huntington remarked that he was the strangest person that ever was and he could not understand where he went, but he had shown them the Gospel in a new light.

"Mother Huntington felt that this stranger was some messenger from heaven and all the family were deeply impressed with his wonderful influence and beautiful way of explaining the scriptures."

"When the Gospel of life and salvation was brought to them by Hyrum Smith and other Elders, they seemed to coincide with what the stranger had told them concerning the Bible and the restoration of the Gospel. All the family but one accepted the Gospel and prepared to emigrate in a few years to Kirtland; here they met the Prophet of God, Joseph Smith, and became his faithful and loyal followers and friends."

"On an occasion when the Prophet Joseph was speaking of the three Nephites, Brother Huntington related this little incident to him. He laid his hand on his head and said: 'My dear brother, that man was one of the Three Nephites who came to prepare you for the restoration of the Gospel and its acceptance."

"Many incidents of a similar nature occurred, but those were days when the children of men were seeking for guidance in the new and enduring faith which is as old as the world but had been forsaken by men and it was again brought forth by the power of God through His humble servant Joseph Smith." *(While visiting in Portland, Oregon, during the month of September, 1938, Pres. Wm. R. Sloan related the above incident to N.B. Lundwall. Assorted Gems of Priceless Value, 1944. pgs. 20-22.)*

Chapter Eighteen

The Right Road

Rose Ann Gubler Hafen

I have listened to Rose Ann Horsley Ensign tell this story a number of times, when I was a young girl.

One time, while crossing the plains, she got too far behind before she noticed, and when she decided to follow the company of ox teams, they were no longer in sight. Of course she thought she would follow the road and soon catch them. This was all right as long as there was just one road to follow. Finally she came to where the road was divided, each one leading in a different direction. She didn't know what to do. She finally decided to take the one which was traveled the most. She had no sooner started down the road than a man dressed in a gray suite stood there directing her which way to go. He pointed to the opposite road she was traveling and said, "This is your road!" She was very frightened and confused at this incident and thought this man was trying to mislead her, so she continued down the road she had started, almost on a run. Again,

64

in a very loud, firm voice, he said, "I tell you this is your road!" It frightened her so much that she was afraid to disobey him, and took the road he had pointed out to her. After she had gone a short distance, she turned around to see which direction the stranger had taken, but he was no longer in sight. She never knew where he came from or where he went and never saw him again. She has often thought perhaps he was one of the Three Nephites, because she found her company safely without further delay or harm. *(Heart Throbs of the West, by Kate B. Carter. Daughters of Utah Pioneers. 1941. Vol. 3, pg. 352.)*

Chapter Nineteen

An English Newspaper

Margaret McNeil Ballard

On May 17, 1884, the Logan Temple was dedicated. My husband, Henry Ballard, being Bishop, was very busy writing out recommends to all who wished to go to the Temple, when my daughter, Ellen, came in with a newspaper in her hand and asked to see her father. I told her that he was very busy and to give the paper to me and I would give it to him after awhile. She said, "No, a man gave the paper to me and told me to give it to no one but my father." I let the child take the paper to her father, and when he took it and looked at it he was greatly surprised for he saw that the paper had been printed in his birthplace, Newberry Berkshire England, just four days before. He was so amazed at such an incident that he called Ellen to him and asked her where the man was who had given her the paper. She said she was playing on the sidewalk with other children when two men came down the street, walking in the middle of the road. One of the men called to her, saying "Come here, little girl." She hesitated at first for there were other little girls with her. Then he pointed to her and said "You." She went to him and he gave her the paper and told her to give it to no one but her father, without asking who her father was. The paper contained a column entitled "Graveyard Gleanings," and marked with a blue pencil. This contained about sixty names of dead friends and acquaintances of my husband, including his old school teacher, giving dates of birth and death. Brother Ballard took the paper to the President of the Temple and asked him what he thought about it.

Brother Merrill said, "Brother Ballard, that was one of the Three Nephites, or some other unusual person, who brought that paper to you, for it could come in no other way in so short a time." The paper is now in the Church Historian's office in Salt Lake City. *(Autobiography of Margaret McNeil Ballard.)*

Chapter Twenty

My Automobile Accident

Josephine Jarvis Reay

During the month of August 1968 in Salt Lake City, I was on the way to the University Hospital driving my sister, Flora Morrison, whose son was in the hospital. I had forgotten something I had planned to take to my hospitalized nephew, so upon returning to my home to pick up the gift, I was driving through a school zone when a drunk driver ran the stop sign. He collided broadside into my driver's side door entering into my car almost 2 feet knocking me across the car and out the passenger side door where I landed up against a steel, chain-link fence and the metal fence post was imbedded in my face.

After being transported to the hospital myself, the doctors told my daughter that I wouldn't live, and she started to make funeral arrangements. There was no insurance to pay for a single intensive care room and so the hospital staff had to move me to a four bed ward with other patients.

I was an ordinance worker in the Salt Lake Temple at the time and the Temple President and my Stake President had both been in at different times to administer to me and give me a blessing, as well as other priesthood brethren from my home ward. Nothing seemed to be doing any good in the way of healing my critical condition because every time they would move me, I would go into shock. I had nine ribs broken, three breaks in my pelvis and a serious spinal injury. The spinal injury made it impossible to move me, even slightly, or I would be traumatized.

Two weeks later, at night in the hospital, I had two "missionary looking" men visit me. One was a tall blonde fellow with blue eyes and a strong jaw. The other gentleman was shorter and had a darker complexion.

The Sunday night that the two strangers appeared in the doorway of my hospital room, they asked the lady in the front bed where Josephine Jarvis was. Now Josephine Jarvis was my maiden name and I was not known to anyone at that time by that name. The other patient said, she didn't know a Josephine Jarvis but, pointing to me, she said, "her name is Josephine." They walked up to the bed and said that they were there to give me a blessing and I told them that I had been administered to already a number of times. The two said that they had been sent to give me a "special blessing" and so I agreed.

The tall blond one stepped to the head of the bed and laid his hands upon my head and the other one pulled the curtain around the bed for more privacy. I was given a very strange and wonderful blessing. As he spoke, he gave the blessing under the authority of the "restored Melchizedek Priesthood" and the specific wording he used, I have never heard in my entire life. He promised that I would be healed and that I was to go about my normal workday as the Lord had a special mission for me. The whole blessing reassured me that I would have no lingering disabilities from the accident injuries. After the blessing, they pulled back the curtain and proceeded to leave the room. The night nurse that was assigned to me and that was on duty at that time was one of the temple proxies in Salt Lake who came to the temple quite often and I knew her well. I asked her if she had seen the two visitors, or if anyone had asked to see me, and she said "no".

I asked another lady in the room who was a sister to one of the ordinance workers at the temple if she had seen anyone and she said that she had seen the curtains drawn closed, but that she had seen no one. They keep track of any and all visitors, and especially during non visiting or nighttime hours in the hospital, and no one saw these two brethren. They just walked out the door and disappeared!

The next morning, my Stake President visited and after hearing my episode and excitement, he verified that my visiting disciples "were two of the Nephites who were left on the earth to minister" and to be careful who I tell the incident to as disbelievers may scorn my testimony.

Three days later, I was miraculously healed and was up walking around my hospital room. With injuries and breaks to my backbone, my ribs and my pelvis, I was up and about walking! This occurred in the L.D.S. Hospital in Salt Lake City, Utah, in August of 1968. I testify to you that these glorious visitors were two of the Three Nephites and that they are here on the earth performing their assigned missionary labors for our Saviour, as he commanded. I have always strived to fulfill the promises the Lord gave to me when the Nephites blessed me and restored my life. *(Recorded in personal interview by Douglas Beardall on Nov. 2, 1992.)*

Chapter Twenty-One

"*Your Baby Is Not Going To Die*"

When two years of age, I became very ill with acute meningitis. My body was so badly drawn that the back of my head and my feet were touching. My family had called in five of the leading physicians of New Orleans, and all pronounced the case hopeless. One afternoon my father was standing on the lawn in front of the hotel talking with some of the boarders when a well-dressed man with skin so fair it was almost transparent appeared before him and asked if he had any work he could do. Then he said, "I understand that you have a very sick child." And in the course of the conversation he asked to see me. He seemed so concerned that my father had all confidence in him in the sick room."

That was all he said about my condition at the time, but he kept in very close contact. He set to work about the place . . . but he would never accept money.

He said that he had no need of money. . . . One evening, after Mr. Osburn [the stranger] had been at our home several days, the doctor called the family together and told them that I would not live through the night. After the doctor had hurried away, Mr. Osburn came and stood at the door of my room and said, "Don't grieve. Your baby is not going to die. I have communed with the other world and she cannot go. She has a work here that no one else can do. She will pass the crisis tonight and you will all see an improvement in the morning." One day while my father was in New Orleans, Mr. Osburn vanished.

I had not heard the story until some time after we had met some of the Mormon elders and our family had been converted. When I finally asked my mother to come and be baptized with me, she told me this story and stated that this was the answer to the stranger's statement that I was spared for a work that no one else could do.

Q: Did he ever tell you that he was one of the Nephites? Or that he was connected with the Mormon Church in any way?

A: No, he didn't. This incident wasn't connected with any of the Mormon beliefs until years later when we happened to relate the story to some Mormon elders. Of course, it strengthened our faith in the Church to learn that similar events had occurred to others who believed in the Church.

Q: You really did get well soon after his visit?

A: I had no after-effects at all from my illness. I recovered quite rapidly after that night, and I haven't been ill to speak of since that time. *(The Three Nephites, by Hector Haight Lee. The University of New Mexico. 1949. pgs. 142-143.)*

Chapter Twenty-Two

A Nephite Visits A Descendant Of The Lamanites

Laura Angell King

An old man, John Alexander Tims, who will be ninety-six years old on July 15, next, lives in the little town of Kirtland, New Mexico, with his daughter, Rachel Harris. He is not a pioneer of Utah, nevertheless he has spent his days in service and received much joy from loyalty to his Church.

Brother Tims was born in Chester County, South Carolina, July 15, 1845. He is one-eighth Catawba Indian. He fought in the Civil War in the Confederate Army, and was a sharpshooter. His story of an incident while he lived in South Carolina is as follows:

"One morning, just as the family was sitting down to breakfast, a knock came at the door. Upon opening it, a strange man stood there. He was invited in, seemed in a great hurry, but the purpose of his visit was to deliver a message. He told Alexander Tims that two missionaries would come to his home, and that he would know who they were. Then the stranger left. At the time, Brother Tims did not realize just who this visitor was, but after the two promised missionaries (two Mormon Elders) visited the family, bringing the Book of Mormon with them, he learned of the Three Nephites, and it dawned on him that the morning visitor might have been one of these. He has always felt that this being was sent to open up the way for the introduction of missionary work in South Carolina. *(Heart Throbs of the West, by Kate B. Carter. Daughters of Utah Pioneers. 1941. Vol. 3, pg. 359.)*

Chapter Twenty-Three

Two Nephites Blessed Me

Sarah Hutchinson Eccles Baird

My Father, William Eccles, was born April 6, 1825, in Dumbartonshire, Scotland; was baptized into The Church of Jesus Christ of Latter-day Saints, April 5, 1842, when he was less than 17 years old.

In 1843 he married Sarah Hutchinson, at Paisley, Renfrewshire, Scotland. In 1863 he emigrated to Utah, bringing with him his wife, and seven children.

I was born December 31, 1854 in Glasgow, Lanoshire, Scotland. I have five brothers and one sister as follows: John, Stewart, William, David, Margaret, and Samuel. Many are the good times we had together as children. Mother and Father were very poor and we had a hard time, which made us remember our happy times with much appreciation.

When I was eight and one-half years of age, my Father brought the family to America. Father was blind then, and he met the difficulties of traveling with much less vigor than if he could have seen. Our cousins (mother's side) came with us, so we had quite a large family. Everything was so strange and new to me that I can't recall the ocean nor the ship we traveled on. Mother had a load on her hands.

The day we were to see land we thrilled with excitement as we sighted America. We had rolled across the briny deep for many days, and the sight of land was indeed welcome to our eyes. On landing we stayed in the eastern states for some time until we could get a train to take us out west to the Mormon settlements. My cousins James, John and Stewart Moise all liked the East very much, and if we had not planned to come to Utah they might have stayed there.

We got a train to bring us out west and decided to live in Eden, Ogden Valley, Utah, where we settled and lived quite happily for about three years. About this time my cousins became discontented and wished very much to return to the eastern states where they could obtain better work and also make more money. Father was quite disturbed that they did not have enough faith in their religion to stay with it through hardships and trials, but they were determined. They all talked persuasively to Father to get his consent, so Father said he would have to sleep on it and tell the boys the next morning. After much thought and deliberation, Father decided to take us all to Oregon City and the Moise boys could get work in the woolen factories and we would not be so far from Eden. The boys agreed to this arrangement.

For a number of days we were all very busy packing our things to go. All father had to travel in was a cart with a yoke of cattle, but our faith gave us hope and strength. The Moise boys got a wagon and a yoke of cattle and we started off. Father decided to take the Old Oregon Trail, which would take us through the Cascade Mountains which would be very beautiful. It was early in April when we started out and we had a full three months journey before us. The only chance we would have to see other people would be at pony express stations which we would come to from time to time, and about twenty miles apart were the home stations where the cattle would get fed and rested.

The first incident that I remember were the Indians, they had just killed a large family, and we shuddered as we thought of what we had just been saved. It must have been only three days previous to our coming that their graves were covered over. As we slept that night, the wolves and coyotes howled from out of the darkness, we felt a great sympathy for that family who surely had loved each other as we did, and had met such a ghastly fate. We would have been grateful for a camp fire that night, but the light would attract the Indians, and there were only the twelve of us which would be small prey for a tribe of Indians. The dawn was welcome the next day, although it meant hours of walking over a hot trail with the sun pouring down from above.

When we came to the next pony express station we camped to get food and water and rest. We were all very tired and the cattle needed food. Everybody there called Father "Captain" and would marvel at his endurance at traveling with just the two families of us on the lonely and perilous trail. This reminded us of Brigham Young's words that we would never see an Indian, and we had not seen one on our journey so far.

After traveling some distance we entered the Cascade Mountains and had a long, long journey ahead of us. It seemed as though mountains were everywhere, though we traveled and traveled. After three days we came out on a high plateau and saw a great cloud of smoke rolling up toward us. Father said Indians must have set the whole mountain afire to drive out the wild animals for food. It was an awful sight. The smoke came toward us in great clouds and it was everywhere. This was an unexpected obstacle in our journey, but there was nothing to do but go through the great fire the best we knew how. The animals were greatly frightened and would hardly go on with us. The ground was hot and the trees crashed to the earth with thunderous rolls. The boulders were hot and the burning tree stumps were all about us. Many times we would burn our feet and hands in helping the cattle go forward, or in hauling the wagon over the hot rocks and tree trunks. The cattle would step on the hot rocks and bellow the most pitiful tones and we were burning ourselves as well as they. If a tree had fallen across our cart then, it would have burned it and everything inside. It seemed that this fire would never end. The shoes were burned off our feet and we had to stand on the hot earth and stones to help the cattle onward.

We were indeed grateful to see the end of the mountains as it meant the end of the fire for us. But there was still another obstacle in our path. On our roadway was a large rock, and carved on it were the words, "The straight way to hell." The carver had given the pathway a very characteristic name as it was nearly perpendicular. In order to proceed further, we all got out of the cart and wagon and the boys tied trees on the back of them and locked the wheels and we got down after much care and labor. As we descended, the way was so steep that but for the trees, the wagons would surely have rolled down and been crushed into heaps of dust and broken wood. How glad we were to find water and a camping place a little distance from the end of our steep trail. We ate and rested for a short while and then went on to a home pony express station.

The cattle's feet were severely burned, so we camped at this station for three days in order to cure them, also to feed and rest them. It was good to camp for a while after traveling steadily through the mountains and through the fire and down the steep ravine. We had a campfire and hot food and water and this was a safe place from the Indians. We rested near our fire at night and the wolves howling in the distance seemed further away because of the cheerful blaze. We all regained hope and faith as well as physical rest and food and were ready to start onward to Oregon City by the third day.

Success and prosperity was with us in Oregon City, for my cousins got work in a woolen factory and my brother and father got work in the mountains cutting wood for the factory. It was mighty good to have the men working and we settled in a small cabin and kept house for them. This life was very sweet after the lonely and fearful days on the trail.

We had been there about two years when my brother David went to Puget Sound and made quite a raise of money. While he was gone our family moved to Salem, and father cut loads of cord wood for the people to burn as fuel, while my cousins stayed in Oregon City. Father and Mother went down to see them when the two years time for staying in Oregon was almost up, to see if they were preparing to go back to Salt Lake, and to discuss plans for the journey with them. It was a great surprise and disappointment to Father and Mother when the boys said they would not go back; that they would stay right there because they were making good money in the factory, and were getting along fine. They even told Father to stay away with his preaching, and that they would not listen. Father and Mother were quite hurt at these words, but Father met the issue by telling James, in spite of his evident unwillingness to listen that they would be glad to return to Utah.

Father and Mother came home with sorrow in their hearts at the boys failure to keep their promise to return in two years, and their lack of faith in their religion, and longing for the spirit of religion that we would find on returning to Utah.

Two weeks later a telegram came to us from Oregon City saying Mrs. Moise was very sick and asking for Father and Mother to come with all speed; that she was so sick the doctors had given up hope of saving her life. Father and Mother went down immediately and found auntie extremely sick with spotted fever. The doctor could not cure her and even said she would not live. The boys were grief stricken and were wailing for help and comfort. Everyone was thankful to see Father and Mother had come after the boys had talked to them and the boys begged Father to tell them how to save their Mother's life. Father said they could not expect the Lord to have mercy on them after the way they had talked about Brigham Young, and the only thing they could do was to get down on their knees and ask His forgiveness of their sin; if they would do this with repentance in their hearts, they would see a change in their Mother's condition. The boys were only too glad to save their Mother's life, so they prayed as Father had directed. Father sent out and got a bottle of olive oil and blessed and administered to her, and prayed for her. After this, a peaceful sleep came over her and she slept soundly all night. We were thankful to see her sleep, for she had not been able to sleep for many nights, but had tossed in a high fever all the time.

When Father was sure of her regaining her health, he returned to Salem, while Mother stayed and took care of her. With the good care that Mother administered and the renewed faith of God that prevailed in that house, she improved steadily and when she was well enough to travel, David came home from Puget Sound, and we got ready to start back to Eden, Utah.

Father had been preaching the Gospel to the people who lived around us and when we decided to go, two men wished to travel with us and hear Father's teachings while on the trail. So we got a wagon with a double wagon box and two yoke of cattle and horses and a cow. The Moise boys got a span of horses and we started out. We decided to take the trail that would take us through the Blue Mountains instead of the Cascade, which we crossed in going to Oregon. Our return traveling would be much easier than the going had been, because we had more animals and also a better vehicle. We were very cheerful and hopeful, too, because we were returning to see old friends, Brigham Young, and the old scenes that had become dear to our hearts.

I remember one time, we came to the home pony express station and stopped to change hands around, and rest the cattle and horses for a few minutes. The men there told Father that about ten miles further there was a little ravine with a stream of pure water that would furnish us with water and refreshment, but for fifteen miles further there would be nothing for the cattle to eat or drink.

So Father decided to camp at the station as we were tired and hungry and ten miles in those days were many miles of traveling. So we got washed and fixed dinner, everyone was hungry, and it was a good thing, as our meals were very simple. The Moise boys stopped their wagon a little distance away and we all sat down and ate heartily. After eating, when David and I were helping Mother with the dishes, I suddenly felt the presence of someone behind us, looking around there were two men coming toward us. I told David in a quiet but excited voice about them. Mother heard me and asked in a fearful voice if they were Indians, but I told her they were not. David helped Mother out of the wagon and she greeted them courteously, as they were two white men, evidently traveling together around the country. They were dressed in the usual style, such as Father wore, but they could not speak or understand

English. They pointed to their mouths and then to the food, meaning they were hungry.

Mother asked David what to give them as we only had some cooked apples, bread and crust coffee. David said the only thing to do was to share what we had, so we set places and food for them. They ate and seemed to enjoy their meal though it was so simple.

When they had finished they came over to Mother, and one of them handed Mother some money out of his pocket. Mother would not take it though, and tried to show them that they were welcome to the food they had eaten, and to more of it if they wished. She patted him on the shoulder and told him to keep it as someone else might want it some day and they would need it.

When they understood they came close to Mother and one put his hand on her head and they both gave Mother a blessing in a foreign tongue. We were all awed by this action, and when they left, my Sister Margaret and I ran up a little incline to see which way they had gone. Although the country was flat and barren, we could see for miles, neither of us could see them and this astonished us greatly. We were quick to spread the news that Mother had a blessing in a foreign tongue from two white men. We expected that our Aunt and the boys would have seen the men, as they passed right by their wagon when I saw them, but none of our cousins had seen them.

We forgot this blessing, and parts of the language the man had used; fifteen years later, while living in Eden, Cache Valley, Mother had an opportunity to relate this experience. Eliza R. Snow was having a Relief Society meeting at Huntsville, at which her two counselors were present. Mother was invited to this meeting, but was afraid to leave me home alone to take care of the house for so long a time. I persuaded her that I could take care of myself and the house, so she went. Mother was very glad to go and enjoyed the meeting very much. After the meeting, Miss Snow promised those present a treat, so she brought out Brother Joseph Smith's watch and everybody was alive with interest and handled it with great care. Then she said she would let them hear Mother Eve's tongue and she spoke to them in Mother Eve's language, which was very sweet to hear and very interesting. Then she said she would let them hear the Nephite tongue, and she spoke to them in the Nephite language. When she got through speaking, Mother went up to her and said that she knew every word she had spoken. The people were astonished, but Mother told them about these two men who had blessed her on the trail homeward, and that they had spoken the same language that Miss Snow had used. Then Miss Snow put her hands upon Mother's shoulders and told her that she was indeed a blessed woman, as these were Two Nephite brethren who had blessed her. *(Submitted by David Wright, October 30, 1992.)*

Chapter Twenty-Four

An Indian Legend

N. A. Jensen

The following Indian legend as told to N.A. Jensen, Mesa, Arizona, by an old Indian of the Pima tribe, Casa Grande, Arizona, 1922, is very significant viewed in the light of the Book of Mormon account of Christ's visit to the Nephites:

"Long, long time 'go heap big cloud come up east sky, no rain. Sun go down, no dark. Sun come up, shine behind cloud. Sun go down, 'gin, no dark. Big cloud make light. Sun come up 'gin. All my people heap 'fraid, fall on ground, no look up. Hear big noise behind cloud. People heap more 'fraid. Big tommyhawk in sky cut cloud open, no rain. People heap more 'fraid. Hear big song in sky, people look up, see white chief walk on cloud, sing fine song. Lot other white chiefs make big long ladder reach up cloud. Big white chief come down ladder. Indians all lay down face on ground. Big Chief take all Indian papooses up on cloud. Indians all cry, wash off war paint, break bows, take feathers off. Big white chief bring fine, white blankets, put on my people. Tell heap long story. Papooses eat up all chief's bread. Big chief make more bread, feed 'em all my people, heap full. Big chief make all my people wash in big water, make 'em white like Big Chief. Big Chief take 'em three Indian chiefs ride on cloud. No see' em all day. Indian chiefs come back, heap white, like Big Chief. Big Chief sleep behind cloud. Some day wake 'em up, come down here, stay with Indians, be Indian Big Chief, give 'em white blankets, heap big corn, no more fight."

Chapter Twenty-Five

My Nephite Visitor

C. Edwards

The following circumstance transpired at my home in the Seventeenth Ward, one-half block north of where now stands President George Q. Cannon's house, in April 1852:

I had been to the morning meeting at the Bowery with Sister Dunsdon, she and her little daughter were living with me at this time. My husband was sick at home and in bed. Little Jane, for this was the girl's name, had been left at home to look after my husband's welfare until I should return. As soon as the service was over, I and Sister Dunsdon hastened home. We had scarcely removed our shawls when a knock came at the door. I said, "Come in." The door opened, and to my surprise there stepped in an aged looking gentleman, tall and grave, his hair as white as wool and combed behind his ears so as to hang down his shoulders. He wore a felt hat. His pants and coat were dark and considerably worn. His shoes were new, but I noticed that he wore no stockings. His thin features were lit up with a very pleasant smile. When he had entered he said, "Oh! can I have a dinner here today?"

I said, "Yes, indeed! If you can make a dinner of such as I have, you are welcome to it, but I have nothing but bread that I can give you."

I then remembered I had some few onions and I asked him if he would like some.

He answered, "I would."

I had previously asked him to take a seat. I placed a white cloth on the table, a plate, knife and fork, a glass of water, a plate of bread and a little white dish with four onions. This was the best I could do.

When I had laid the table he turned round to face the table and proceeded to eat. I thought by the way he ate that he must be very hungry.

When he was through he arose from the table, and putting his hand into his pockets said, "What do you charge me for my dinner today?"

I could but smile at the thought of charging for so meager a fare, and said, "Nothing. I am only sorry that I have nothing better to set before you."

With this he said, as he rattled the money in his pocket, "I have plenty of money, and can pay you."

With this he took two or three steps in a measured way towards me, and said, "Well, if you charge me nothing for my dinner, may God bless you, and peace be with you."

There was a power in the voice that I never felt before. I was so overcome by it that my very limbs gave way, and I dropped into my chair. He left, and I told Sister Dunsdon to look after him, to see where he was going. In a minute he had disappeared, as though he had left the earth, and not a trace of him could be seen. In those early days there were no houses, not even an outhouse, nor fence of any kind to intercept the eye, and this made us marvel.

I arose myself as soon as my strength returned but not a thing of him could I see, nor have I seen him since, so far as I know.

But now comes a part of my great surprise, for on turning to clear the table so that we might have a little food ourselves, lo it was all there as I had put it.

This visit of the stranger made a very deep impression on my heart, that has never left me to this day. Some time after this Brothers C. C. Rich and Carrington came to us, as my husband was so very sick. I told them of this visit, and Brother C. C. Rich said, "Sister Edwards, do you know who he was?"

I said, "I do not."

"Well," said Brother Rich, "this was one of the ancient Nephites come to help you in your trouble." Brother Rich knew that I had already seen some trouble.

Afterwards, I met the Prophet Heber C. Kimball and he said the same as Brother Rich had said. Then I enquired no longer in my mind as to who the stranger was. The disguise had been torn away, and my poor heart was made to rejoice exceedingly in that a messenger of God had condescended to grace my humble home with his presence and to bless me there.

All who were here at the time of the famine and are now living remember but too well, how I suffered. I had neighbors all around me who passed three and four weeks without a mouthful of bread. I have administered food to mothers whose babies nursed nothing but blood from their breasts. And to many I gave a little flour and bread, and fed many at my table, yet the Lord in all the famine provided for my family.

I gave in the day of my poverty, of the scanty store I had to the man of God, and it seems that ever after, my meal sack never went empty. The stranger said," May God bless you and peace be unto you."

(Juvenile Instructor, Vol. 28:312-313.)

Chapter Twenty-Six

Rescued From A Mob

Glen J. Brown

Incident encountered by my father, George E. Brown, and John J. Oldroyd, over twenty-five years ago. This incident occurred on the Island of Vancouver, B.C.

Five years prior to this incident, two "Mormon" elders had been accused of criminally assaulting a young woman on the Island of Vancouver. For some reason they were proven guilty of the charge and sentenced according to the law of the Island. (The Church, as well as the missionaries who were involved, believed that the act was purposely committed by enemies of Mormonism who arranged the evidence in such a way that it was possible to convict the Mormon elders).

One evening they [Brown and Oldroyd] decided to hold a street meeting. They knew feeling was running high and that they would probably be molested, but they decided to go ahead regardless. They had little more than started when down the street marched a large group of men and boys carrying several large pots of melted tar and several old feather ticks. The leader walked directly to my father and asked him if he was a Mormon. Much to the satisfaction of the mob, my father answered him in the affirmative.

Some of the members of the mob began to tear open the feather ticks, while others stirred the still warm tar. Just as the mob leader and two or three of the mobsters began to tear the clothes from my father's body, a white haired gentleman (no one saw him arrive at the scene) grasped the leader by the wrists and said in a loud commanding voice, "I have heard these boys preach back in the old country and they are all right. Now let them alone."

At this the mob leader showed signs of wanting to fight. (The mob leader was a huge, muscular type of man). Immediately the newcomer grasped him at the nape of the neck with one hand and by the belt with the other and shook him so soundly, taking him completely off his feet, that when he had finished the mobster could not stand without assistance. Members of the mob picked him up, gathered up their feathers and tar and departed much faster than they had appeared.

My father and his companion thanked the white haired man for what he had done and asked him to stay and attend the remainder of the meeting. He accepted their invitation and stood directly in front of them throughout the services. Mr. Oldroyd closed the meeting with prayer, as was the custom, and then looked at the spot where the man had been standing. It was vacant. This was before anyone in the crowd had moved at all. No one had seen him go, not even the people who had been standing at his side.

As I understand it, the Nephites are supposed to be able to appear and disappear at will; on this, was based the conclusion that he might have been one of those Three. *(Manuscript by Glen J. Brown, Scipio, Utah. May 24, 1938.)*

Chapter Twenty-Seven

Three Old Nephites

Orson Pratt

In a sermon delivered in Conference to the Saints assembled in the New Bowery on April 7, 1855, Pratt said:

How pleasant — how glorious it would be, if we had proved ourselves in all things; if we had become pure in heart . . . . Yes; how pleasing — how glorious it would be, could we see the Three Old Nephites whose prayers have ascended up, for something like 1800 years, in behalf of the children of men in the last days, and have them return to their old native land, and find the kingdom of God prepared and pure to receive them, and could we hear their teachings, and their voices lifted up in our midst.

Then let us wake up, and be assured that just as soon as we prepare ourselves for these blessings, so soon they will be upon our heads. Do you suppose that these Three Nephites have any knowledge of what is going on in this land? They know all about it; they are filled with the spirit of prophecy. Why do they not come into our midst? Because the time has not come. The very reason they do not come amongst us is, because we have a work to do preparatory to their coming; and just as soon as that is accomplished they are on hand, and also many other good old worthy ancients that would rejoice our hearts could we behold their countenances, and hear them recite over the scenes they have passed through, and the history of past events, as well as prophecy of the events to come. How great and how precious are the promises of the Lord, contained in ancient revelation! *(Orson Pratt, "Progress of the Work . . . Sanctification of the Saints," Journal of Discourses, II. 1855. pp. 263-264.)*

Chapter Twenty-Eight

A Dream Come True

Nicholas G. Morgan and
Arthur Richardson

The name of the town in which he set up his headquarters belied the greatness of the work he was soon to accomplish; it was called Dirt Town. Its central location to both the large settlements and the small ones made it ideal for his work. Rome, Georgia was one of the larger settlements.

One day, not long after his arrival, he set out for Rome with the intent of holding a meeting. While on the way it dawned on him that he had forgotten to notify the people of his coming. Nevertheless, he trudged on feeling rather sorry for himself for being so negligent. Soon his mind was taken up with thoughts of Civil War experiences for this very road was one over which he had traveled at times as a Union soldier; it was one of the main highways which ran from Chattanooga to Rome, Georgia.

A tree in a fork in the road brought him out of

his revery. For a moment he was uncertain as to which road in the fork would lead him to Rome and while meditating there came to his memory a dream he had had one night, ten years before while residing in the home of Bishop Heywood of the 17th Ward in which he saw this very fork in the road that now lay before him. In the dream, however, he saw President Brigham Young, who, standing in the fork, advised him that the right hand fork would lead him to Rome, but if he would take the left hand fork it would lead him to an experience that would be proof sufficient to him of the divinity of the Gospel of Jesus Christ, as taught by The Church of Jesus Christ of Latter-day Saints.

John remembered he had remarked to Sister Heywood, "I'm not looking for evidences of the divine authenticity of your church, but, I still would like to know what you think of that dream."

To Sister Heywood the matter was not to be lightly treated. "I can give you the interpretation!" She prophesied: "Some day you will join our Church. You will be sent on a mission for our Church. You will be going over the same road you saw in your dream and will come to that identical fork in the road. You will recognize that tree. Brigham Young will not be there, but don't forget what he told you. Act upon his counsel."

Now, here he was! Just as he had dreamed ten years before that he would be! Traveling along the forest road as a missionary; confused as to which road to take. Remembering Sister Heywood's advice to follow the counsel of Brigham Young, he took the left fork of the road which led him into a place, which, surprisingly, was called Haywood Valley.

As he came out of the woods, there spread before him, was a beautiful valley clothed in autumn finery. He felt he had never beheld a scene more lovely. No longer did he fret over not having gone to Rome for his meeting. He took it all as a providential part of this experience. He was tingling with anticipation, and felt that something very important was about to happen — that the promise given him in his dream was about to be fulfilled. He quickened his pace. At a turn in the road he met a man from whom he made some inquiries. He found that Haywood Valley had some twenty-five families of thrifty farmers. He felt a deep urge to stop at the first home he came to. The lady of the house answered. When he had explained his mission he was invited in and made welcome. It was late afternoon. The head of the house had just returned from the fields. Supper was prepared and Elder Morgan was invited to join in the family meal. After supper and evening chores the family gathered in the front room where, by invitation, Gospel subjects were discussed. He was blessed with great freedom of expression as he made plain the truths of the Bible, the first principles, and the plan of salvation prepared by God for the redemption of His children. Before they knew it the midnight hour arrived.

Elder Morgan was invited to spend the night but before concluding the evening's religious feast, the father brought out the family Bible and opened it to the scriptures Elder Morgan had been reading and explaining. Every reference and quotation he had used in his evening's presentation of the Gospel plan was underscored in red in this old family Bible.

As the father proceeded to point to passage after passage marked in red, he had difficulty in suppressing the excitement he felt as he went on to relate that a stranger had visited them about ten days before. They did not know from whence he came. They did not know his name or where he went upon leaving them. They did know that he was neatly dressed and possessed of a most pleasant personality. This stranger spent some time with them and marked numerous passages of scripture in the Bible. Then, strangest of all, he had told them that within a few days another man would visit them to explain in detail and with great clearness the meaning of the marked scriptures and the purpose of this life and eternal life.

Though John Morgan was amazed, yet he was prepared for just such a situation. His faith had increased from the moment he found himself before the fork in the road and had recollected his dream and its interpretation by Sister Haywood many years before. Here was the miraculous incident which Brigham

Young had said would give him additional evidence as to the divinity of the Book of Mormon.

To Elder Morgan, the stranger to whom the head of the house was referring was none other than one of the Three Nephites who were chosen and blessed by the Savior during one of his visits to the western continent to the end that they should never taste of death, but should "live to behold all the doings of the Father unto the children of men, even until all things shall be fulfilled, according to the will of the Father, when I shall come in my Glory, with the powers of heaven."

Before retiring that night, on bended knee, and in the spirit of deep humility, he thanked God for this great testimony that had been given him and promised that from then on he would dedicate all his talents and possessions to this work of saving souls and bringing to pass the purposes of the Almighty on the earth.

The first thing he did the next morning was to send a letter to Rome advising a friend there that it might be some time before he would get to that city as he had much work to accomplish in Haywood Valley, but when he had concluded it he would visit with them.

From his kindly benefactors he obtained the names of the various families living in the valley. He set about the ministry that lay before him. For the next month he devoted every waking hour to the teaching of the people, visiting every home in the valley. He found to his utter amazement that, with the exception of one or two cases, the stranger had visited every family, marking their Bibles and assuring them that shortly another would come who would explain the Gospel to them in its fullness. Every family thus visited by the stranger was converted and baptized into the Church by Elder Morgan, including the Methodist minister.

His church building became the meeting house for the new converts and he, himself, became the Presiding Elder of the Haywood Branch. — January 20, 1877. *(The Life and Ministry of John Morgan, by Arthur Richardson and Nicholas G. Morgan, Sr. 1965. pgs. 119-123.)*

Chapter Twenty-Nine

The Miraculous Healing

Asa L. Dickson

William Henderson Dickson, born March 22, 1850, Morse, Iowa, was the third son of Billa and Mary Stoddard Dickson. The parents joined the Church and emigrated to Utah in the early sixties, and made their home in Centerville, Davis County, Utah.

"My small companion and I were playing on a haystack; because of the strong winds that blow there, the stack had been propped and held in place by poles propped up with two-tined pitchforks, of which the handles were resting on the ground, and the tines pointing upward. After playing some time, we became tired and decided to get down. I, boy like, thought I would jump off, but in so doing I fell directly on one of the upturned tines. It pierced my body just above the left hip. I hung suspended while my companion ran for help. All of the folks were away from home that day except two young ladies; one of them being tall and strong, succeeded in lifting me down."

"Of course I was very ill for several days, and nothing, it seemed, could be done for me. I was just gradually wasting away, and everyone said that it was impossible for me to live. One day I had been much more restless than usual, and had been carried from room to room several times. Turning on my bed, I saw a man standing in the middle of the room. He was talking to mother, and asking the privilege of administering to me. Mother gladly consented, and offered to go for someone to assist him, but he said he needed no assistance. He came over and knelt down by my bed, and placed his hands on my head and blessed me. Though the words he used have gone from my memory, I shall never forget the feeling that came over me. It was the most blessed, holy feeling I have ever experienced. When he took his hands from my head, I was instantly healed. There were no days or even hours of waiting, for I was entirely well from that time on."

"In appearance, the man was just ordinary, neatly dressed, and a little above the average in height. We do not know where he came from, no one saw him come or go, but we do know that he was sent by the Lord to heal me." *(Heart Throbs of the West, by Kate B. Carter. Daughters of Utah Pioneers. 1941. Vol. 3, pg. 354.)*

Chapter Thirty

Three White Messengers To The Lamanites

Orson Pratt

Forty-five years have passed away since God brought forth this sign, the Book of Mormon, and sent missionaries to the nations — to Tarshish, Pul, Lud, Tubal, Javan, and to the islands afar off, that have not heard his fame neither have seen his glory and these missionaries have declared his glory among the Gentiles. Forty-five years of proclamation to the nations of the Gentiles! Forty-five years of warning to all nations and tongues! Now, after so long a period has elapsed since God brought forth this wonderful sign, He has begun to work among the remnants of the house of Israel, the American Indians, upon this continent, by His own power. What is it that has stirred them up to believe in this work? Has it been your exertion? Not altogether; yet, no doubt, you, in some small degree, as far as your faith would permit, have helped in the work among these wild tribes. You have sought to recover them, you have fed and clothed them to some extent; you have told them occasionally about the records of their fathers; you have tried to bring them to repentance; but after years of labor, you have said — "Alas! alas for them! What can be done to reclaim a people so far fallen into the depths of ignorance and corruption?" Your heart's have been almost discouraged as far as your own labors were concerned. But how soon and how marvelously, when the time had come, has the Lord our God begun to operate upon them as nations and as tribes, bringing them in from hundreds of miles distant to inquire after the Elders of this Church. What for? What do they want with the Elders? They want to be baptized. Who told them to come and be baptized? They say that men come to them in their dreams, and spoke to them in their own language, and told them that away yonder was a people who had authority from God to baptize them; but that they must repent of their sins, cease their evil habits and lay aside the traditions of their fathers, for they were false; that they must cease to roam over the face of the land, robbing and plundering, and learn to live as the white people.

Who are these men who have been to the Indians and told them to repent of their sins, and be baptized by the "Mormons?" They are men who obtained the promise of the Lord, upwards of eighteen centuries ago, that they should be instruments in his hands of bringing about the redemption of their descendants. The Lord God promised them the privilege of working for and in behalf of their descendants in the latter days; and they have begun the work. All this was foretold in this record, the Book of Mormon.

Now these men lived in the first century of the Christian era on this continent; and when that generation all passed away they also lived in the second century of the Christian era, and ministered to the ancient inhabitants on this land. And when the second century had all passed off the stage of action they also lived in the third century; and in the fourth century the Lord took these three men from the midst of the remnant of Israel on this land. Where did he take them? I do not know, it is not revealed. Why did he take them away? Because of the apostasy of the people, because the people were unworthy of the ministration of such great and holy men; because they sought to kill them; because they cast them into dens of wild beasts twice; and these men of God played with those wild beasts as a child would play with a suckling lamb, and received no harm from them. They cast them three times into a furnace of fire, and they came forth therefrom and received no hurt. They dug deep pits in the earth and cast them, therein, supposing that they would perish; but by the power of the word of God that was in them, they smote the earth in the name of the Lord, and were delivered from these pits. And thus they went forth performing signs, wonders and miracles among this remnant of Israel, until their wickedness became so great that the Lord commanded them to depart out of their midst. And the remnant of Israel, from that day to the present — between fourteen and fifteen centuries — have been dwindling in unbelief, in ignorance, and in all the darkness which now surrounds them; but notwithstanding their darkness and misery, the Three Nephites, for many generations, have not administered to them because of the commandment of the Almighty to them.

But are they always to remain silent? Are there no more manifestations to come from these three men? Are they never again to remember the remnants of the House of Israel on this land? Let us read the promise. "Behold I was about to write the names of those who were never to taste of death, the Lord forbade; therefore I write them not for they were hid from the world; but behold I have seen them." Mormon saw them nearly four centuries after they were caught up into heaven, and after they received their partial change. Mormon saw them and they administered unto him. He says — "Behold I have seen them and they have ministered unto me;

and behold they will be among the Gentiles and the Gentiles knoweth them not." They will, no doubt, call them poor deluded Mormons, and say that they ought to be hooted out of society, and that they ought to be presented, afflicted, and hated by all people. "They will be among the Gentiles and the Gentiles knoweth them not. They will also be among the Jews, and the Jews shall know them not. And it shall come to pass that the Lord seeth fit, in his wisdom, that they shall minister unto all the scattered tribes of Israel, and unto all nations, kindreds, tongues and people, and shall bring out of them unto Jesus many souls, that their desire may be fulfilled; and also because of the convincing power of God which is in them; and they are as the angels of God. And if they shall pray unto the Father in the name of Jesus, they can show themselves unto whatsoever man it seemeth them good; therefore great and marvelous works shall be wrought by them before the great and coming day when all people must surely stand before the judgment seat of Christ. Yea even among the Gentiles shall there be a great and a marvelous work wrought by them, before that judgment day."

Now, having read these things, let us come back again to this spiritual movement that we hear of among the remnants of Jacob, in these western deserts, in the northwest hundreds of miles, in the west and in the southwest. It is not confined to hundreds, but thousands testify that men have appeared individually in dreams, speaking their own language and as Brother Hyde said last Tuesday, these men tell their descendants what their duties are, what they should do, and how they should hunt up this people, repent of their sins, be baptized, etc. And the parties who have been thus instructed time and time again, have fulfilled the commandments that they received, and some of them have come hundreds of miles to be baptized, and they are now desirous of laying aside their savage disposition, their roaming habits, and they want to learn to cultivate the earth, to lay down their weapons of war, cease stealing and to become a peaceable good people.

The work thus commenced will not stop here.

(Delivered in the New Tabernacle, Salt Lake City, by Orson Pratt, Sunday Morning, April 11, 1875. Reported by David W. Evans. Journal of Discourses, Vol. 18:19-22.)

Chapter Thirty-One

Never Want For Food

Eunice Steward

"After first settling in Payson I woke up one morning to find the ground covered with several inches of snow. I was busy with my housework in the middle of the morning when a tall dignified elderly gentleman knocked at my door. We were miles away from any neighbors and my husband had been away for a few days."

"I answered the door and invited him into the house. He asked if he might have something to eat. I replied that all I had left in the house was bread and milk but he was welcome to that. He sat by the table while I was preparing the simple fare, but after I had set it before him he ate nothing." He rose and thanked her. He then promised her that she or her family would never want for food. He went out the door, closing it behind him. "I followed him out but he had disappeared. No footprints were found in the

snow. I believe that he was one of the Three Nephites mentioned in the Book of Mormon who were promised eternal life because of their goodness."
(Manuscript version in WPA Writers' Project Files.)

Chapter Thirty-Two

Open Heart Surgery

Josephine Raey

My sister, Flora Jarvis Morrison, has had a number of major open heart surgeries. The operations occurred in the hospital in El Paso, Texas, when Flora was 63 years old, in 1990. One day she was having chest pains and the doctors immediately put her in the hospital because she was having another heart blockage and they would have to operate.

When they were preparing to operate, Flora was left in the hallway outside the operating room while the hospital staff prepared for the surgery. She was laying on the bed in the hallway all by herself when two men approached her there. They asked her what was going to happen and Flora told the strangers that she was preparing for another heart operation. They asked her if she knew what being administered to meant, and she said that she did. We are going to give you a "special blessing."

A sweet calm swept over my sister as nothing previous has ever done; assuring her that the operations would be a success. Flora said that the two visitors appeared "out of nowhere" and just "disappeared" after the blessing. Knowing that individuals dressed in street clothing are not allowed in the surgical wards and rooms of any hospital without sterile uniforms and gowns, made the special experience that much more amazing.

They were not interrupted during the blessing, and no one else saw the disciples who suddenly appeared and then vanished just as quickly as they appeared, never leaving their names. During surgery, the physicians removed a portion of her heart tissue and some of the heart muscle and now my sister Flora is healthier than she has ever been before. Flora testifies that she knows in her heart that the two healers were of the Three Nephites.

As my sister recounted this marvelous experience and testimony to me, it has strengthened my resolve to be a better missionary and messenger of Jesus Christ. I have been on four missions and plan to continue in the same work as the Three Nephites are involved in bringing more souls into the Kingdom of God. *(Transcribed by C. D. Beardall through telephone interview with Josephine Raey, November 1992.)*

Chapter Thirty-Three

Neighbors Saw The Three

Early in June, 1829, a young man drove up to Joseph's door after two days of hard traveling. He said that he had come from Fayette, Seneca Co., New York, one hundred and fifty miles away for the purpose of carrying the Prophet and his companion to Fayette if they wished to go. He was David Whitmer, son of Peter Whitmer, and his father invited Joseph to come to their home. They offered him protection and to provide for his wants while he was working at the translation.

Joseph accepted the invitation and, leaving Emma with her father, he and Oliver departed with David. Before setting out Joseph asked the Lord how he should carry the plates. In answer to his prayer Moroni appeared and took them from him, promising to return them again. When he reached Fayette the angel visited him in Mr. Whitmer's garden and gave them over to him.

The translation continued very rapidly, for when Oliver grew tired, David or his brother John was ready to write at the Prophet's dictation. When not translating, Joseph and Oliver spent their time in teaching those who came to listen and in explaining what the Lord had revealed to them.

There were many serious persons who wished to hear the truth. David Whitmer had been remarkably aided that he might hasten to bring Joseph to Fayette. Three strange men were seen scattering the plaster that David had put in a heap upon one of his fields to fertilize it, and they did it with more than human skill and speed. In harrowing in wheat on another field David had done in one day more than he could usually have done in two or three days. Many in the neighborhood hearing of this were impressed that the Lord had helped him in bringing the two young men and believed that they were His servants.

When any person became convinced that the work was divine and desired to be baptized, the ordinance was performed. Joseph soon had the pleasure of baptizing his brother Hyrum and David Whitmer, and at the same time Oliver baptized Peter Whitmer, Junior. Soon there were so many believers that baptisms were performed nearly every day in Seneca Lake, a beautiful body of water lying on the western border of Seneca County.

While at work on the translation it was learned that three persons should be shown the sacred plates, in order that their testimony might be given to the world. Oliver Cowdery, David Whitmer and Martin Harris begged Joseph to ask the Lord if they could not be the ones. Joseph did this during the month of June, 1829, and the Lord answered that if they trusted in His words with full purpose of heart they should be shown the plates, the breastplate, Urim and Thummim, sword of Laban and the Liahona, or compass, given to Lehi in the wilderness. Soon after they all went into the woods to pray that the Lord would show the plates, which Joseph had given up for the time to the Angel Moroni.

The four men kneeled down and Joseph offered a prayer, then the others in turn prayed, but no answer came. Joseph began again and the others followed but though they prayed with fervor yet they failed to receive any manifestation. Before beginning again Martin Harris said he believed he was the cause of the failure. He offered to go aside and pray alone.

Martin had spoken the truth, for soon after he withdrew, a light of surpassing fairness came down from heaven and within it stood the angel holding the golden plates. He turned the leaves and the characters engraved hereon were illumined so that the witnesses saw them plainly. They also heard the voice of the Lord declaring that the plates before them were revealed by God and had been translated by His power. They were commanded to bear record that the translation was correct.

When the vision passed away Joseph sought Martin Harris. He found him, humbled by this rebuke for his past wickedness and praying with his whole heart for forgiveness and for the privilege of viewing the record. Joseph joined him in prayer and soon the angel again appeared and the whole vision was repeated. Martin had never beheld a spiritual sight before and he could not long bear the glory before him, but he was filled with joy and shouted hosanna to God.

The three men who had been chosen as witnesses drew up and signed a statement, which is now printed in the fore part of the Book of Mormon. They testified to all the world that they had seen an angel holding the plates and heard the voice of God declaring that the translation was correct. Oliver Cowdery, the first signer, went on missions and did much good, but he lost the spirit of the gospel and fell. In 1838 he was cut off the Church. David Whitmer lost his standing at the same time and Martin Harris in the same year. For nine years Oliver Cowdery was separated from the Church, and for thirty-three years Martin Harris remained away, but both were finally rebaptized and died in the Church. David Whitmer never came back, but he and his fellow witnesses affirmed time after time that they had really seen the angel and beheld the golden plates.

The Prophet was permitted to show the record to eight other persons as an additional testimony. They were Christian, Jacob and John Whitmer and Peter Whitmer, Jun., Hiram Page, Joseph Smith, Sen., and his sons Hyrum and Samuel H. Smith. These men handled the plates and seriously judged them to be of gold and engraved with ancient work. They were without exception unflinching in their testimony that the Book of Mormon is true.

When John the Baptist visited Joseph and Oliver to give them the Aaronic Priesthood he promised that the Priesthood of Melchizedek would later be conferred upon them. They became very desirous to receive this and made it a matter of prayer. As they were once asking the Lord about it they heard His voice directing them to ordain each other, but not until they were accepted as spiritual teachers by those already baptized. Sometime after this, during the month of June, 1829, Peter, James and John appeared to them and conferred upon them the Holy Priesthood. These three had been chosen by Jesus Christ when He lived on the earth to preside over the Priesthood and it was their office to restore it when the Lord chose to permit men on the earth again to hold it.

The work of translation was now drawing to an end and a contract was made with Egbert B. Grandin, of Palmyra, to print five thousand copies. In August, 1829, the work of printing began. The copy used was not the original manuscript, but the whole was rewritten and Joseph preserved the original. Three thousand dollars was the price agreed on and Martin Harris gave security for its payment. In March, 1830, the book was issued to the world.

When the work was finished Joseph delivered the sacred treasures to the angel Moroni and left them to be guarded by him. Treasure seekers have

124

searched for them, the stone box has been torn away, but they have been sought in vain and they will remain hidden until the Lord's own due time.

Oliver Cowdery was left by Joseph to watch over the work of printing and the Prophet was free to visit his wife at Harmony. It was, however, a busy winter for him, for he received many revelations concerning the organization of the Church, and he spent much time in declaring the truth to all who would listen. *(The Life of Joseph Smith, The Prophet, by George Q. Cannon. Special Collections. Young People's History of Joseph Smith, pgs. 34-39.)*

Chapter Thirty-Four

The Loaf In The Napkin

At the time of the first settlement of Payson, Utah, a man was sent on a mission to Germany, while the wife was left in Payson to manage their rather isolated farm land. One winter morning, a tall elderly gentleman knocked at her door. Not a little surprised at seeing a stranger in this sparsely populated region she invited him in. He told her he had traveled far and was very hungry. Food was never plentiful in that household, and the fact that it was midwinter caused a greater scarcity than ever. However, the good woman, wrapping part of a loaf of bread in an old bit of peculiarly patterned cloth, offered it to the stranger. The old man thanked her and went his way. The woman followed him to the door and found he had disappeared without leaving a single track in the snow. This incident took place one day before Christmas, and that fact, together with the strangeness of the whole proceeding, caused the young woman to remember the date.

Several years later, the day after her

husband's return, she was helping him to unpack his belongings when she found, carefully folded in a corner of his trunk, the same odd piece of cloth in which she had wrapped the stranger's bread. Her husband related to her this story: "It was on the day before Christmas, the money which was to pay my expenses was many days overdue, and I was alone and penniless in a strange city. I had not eaten for two days and upon looking up I perceived a tall, elderly gentleman walking toward me. I turned aside to allow him to pass, but he took me by the arm, and removing a package from his pocket wrapped in this piece of cloth, placed it in my hand. He then said, 'Go to the post office. Even now your money awaits you there.' Without another word he turned and disappeared around a nearby corner. I opened the package and found it contained a half loaf of fresh bread. Later I went to the post office and found the money, just as he had said." It was the opinion of all who heard the story that the old man who performed this miraculous service could have been none other than one of the Three Nephites. *(Anonymous manuscript in the files of the WPA Writers' Project, Utah State Historical Society, Salt Lake City.)*

Chapter Thirty-Five

The Singing Of A Translated Being

Melvin John Hoggan

During the month of November, 1927, four missionaries (Elders Roy D. Olpin, R. B. Muer, Asahel A. Parry, and Melvin J. Hoggan) of The Church of Jesus Christ of Latter-day Saints were laboring in Medford, Oregon. Elder Parry and I, together with the other two Elders, held street meetings every Saturday evening. On the evening in which this incident happened, Elders Olpin and Muer were absent, having left during the forenoon for Klamath Falls, Oregon, for the purpose of reorganizing the Sunday School at that place. Elder Muer was the senior Elder of the group. Elder Parry had been in the mission field about three months and Elder Hoggan but a month. Both Elders were very inexperienced.

Elder Parry and I were very undecided

whether to hold a street meeting, as we two had never held one before together and only twice with all four Elders present. We had knelt down and had prayed before we left our room which was our usual practice. We walked to the corner of the street in front of one of the banks where we usually held our street meetings. It was rainy and cold. I was not very enthusiastic about holding a meeting, being new in the work. But few persons were on the streets within a radius of many blocks in every direction. I felt that it was perfectly useless to hold a meeting on the street under those conditions. Neither one of us could carry a tune, but we stepped out on the corner and proceeded to sing the song: "Oh My Father." We were just about through the last verse when I noticed a gentleman to the right of me about ten feet away, at the side of an automobile. He was taking off his cap and gloves. He was of a very small build, about five feet eight inches tall, light complexioned, slightly bald, about fifty years of age, and dressed very neatly but not elaborately. He came over to us and asked: "Do you boys mind if I help you sing?" From that time on he took complete charge of the meeting and assumed the responsibility. Elder Parry asked him: "Are you a member of the Church?" The stranger replied by saying: "I am acquainted with this work." He then suggested that we sing: "Love at Home," which was recorded in the small booklet that contained the popular Latter-day Saint songs. One of these small booklets was given to him. We all started to sing this song, but soon Elder Parry and I stopped singing and listened to the beautifully clear tenor voice which rang out for blocks in its sweet harmonious strains. At the time we first started to sing, there were only two or three people listening by the side of the bank building, on the side walk. When he had finished singing this song, a fair sized crowd had assembled, of some twenty persons, which was the largest that had ever gathered in that town before. He stepped to the curb and gave a five minute talk to the people assembled on the theme: "Love at Home." The crowd gave rapt attention while he was speaking, but was less attentive while we spoke to them. After making the very effective remarks, he stated to the crowd: "Now one of the brethren will speak to you," at the same time turning to Elder Parry. Elder Parry then stepped forward and spoke. While Elder Parry was speaking, the stranger stepped up to me and said: "We will sing this song, then you can speak," (pointing to the song numbered 119 in the little booklet, entitled: Glorious Things of Thee are Spoken). I looked at the name of the song and said: "I don't know that song." He replied: "You should, they play it while they pass the sacrament." He then hummed the tune to me, which I afterwards learned was the same tune that was used originally in singing this song, and not the modern tune sometimes used at the present time. While Elder Parry was speaking, several in the crowd were talking which seemed to disturb him. The stranger walked over to them and said something which I did not hear but they were very attentive after he had spoken to them.

After humming the tune of this song to me he turned his face towards the west as though he were looking at some one and said: "Hello," at the same time walking not more than fifteen feet in that direction the crowd being several feet to the north, and all of a sudden he completely vanished from sight. I was watching him closely all the time, observing his actions and taking note of what he said. Elder Parry all this time was talking to the people, and after he had closed his remarks I spoke for a few minutes.

We afterwards walked around the town to see if any individual could be found who coincided with the appearance of this stranger, but no one knew of him before or since. Medford is a town similar to Murray, Utah, with about the same population. When President Sloan visited us in Medford, this incident was related to him and he unhesitantly stated that it was one of the Three Nephites. We were thrilled and amazed at this wonderful experience and will remember it as long as we live. During the visit of this stranger, the feeling experienced was as if a messenger of God was there, sent to assist us with this meeting. A very peaceful and uplifting feeling was experienced and enjoyed. Signed: Melvin John Hoggan. *(Assorted Gems of Priceless Value, N. B. Lundwall. 1944. pgs. 31-33.)*

Chapter Thirty-Six

A Strange Visitor

Mary Harriet Burgess Bullard

Mary Harriet Burgess Bullard was born in Nauvoo, Illinois, in 1842. When she was six years old, she came to Utah with her parents. The following story is taken from her autobiography.

"Early in my married life I was very ill. No hope was held out for my recovery. We could not afford any help so I was in the house alone most of the time.

"One day, while I was lying in bed, a man came to the side of my bed and took hold of my hand and said to me, 'My dear sister, you are very sick. You think you are going to die.' I answered 'yes.' Then he shook his head and said, 'No, the Lord has a great work for you to do. You will live and raise a large family. You shall have power over the Evil One to save the lives of your children and many of the Saints' lives. If you only had faith enough, you could get up right now and dress yourself. Be careful and take care of yourself and you will soon be well and stout."

"I was weak. I closed my eyes and when I opened them he was gone. I rose, put on my clothes and was sitting in the chair when my husband came in. He was surprised and asked, 'Who has helped you dress?' 'Nobody,' I said, 'I've just made up my mind to get well, and I am going to. I am not going to lie in that bed any longer, only when I want to rest."

"At that time, I did not tell anyone of the stranger's visit except my father. He told me it was one of the Three Nephites and that from my description of him, it was the same Nephite which had visited him once when he was ill." *(Heart Throbs of the West, by Kate B. Carter. Daughters of Utah Pioneers. 1941. Vol. 3, pg. 357.)*

Chapter Thirty-Seven

A Nephite Tends the Fire

Mary Miekle

Mary's first story was told to her by a man she said she went with, a returned missionary. And the experience was actually had by this man's missionary companion. He was a man from Montana and the incident occurred during the flu epidemic following the last war. The man's family was ill — very ill. And during the very early hours of the morning he left on foot for the nearest town to get some medicine.

It was in the dead of winter and the trip took him longer than he expected. He returned to see smoke coming out of his chimney, and when he entered, the house was all warm and a meal had been prepared. His mother said a stranger had been there. He had made the fire, and had given them some medicine and prepared some food.

The man looked around outside for any sign of a visitor. There were no marks on the snow that had fallen the night before. There were no signs of a visitor having entered or left the house. He knew the visitor was a Nephite. *(The Three Nephites, by Hector Haight Lee. The University of New Mexico. 1949. Pg. 156.)*

Chapter Thirty-Eight

They Call Me The Wandering Jew

William A. Seegmiller

In the month of November 1867, my parents, William H. and Mary Laidlaw Seegmiller, were married in Salt Lake City. My father and mother were among a number of L.D.S. people who received calls to colonize the southeastern part of Nevada. The group settled on what was known as the Muddy River, in a place called St. Joseph, in the Moapa Valley, Nevada.

Late one afternoon while my father was just outside their tent home chopping wood, he was approached by a rather distinguished-looking person of Jewish type, having a large Roman nose, who accosted father in the German language. Father's parents being German, that language, as well as English, was familiar to him. The visitor asked for something to eat to take along in his bag that he carried across his shoulder, and also for some patches of cloth with which to mend his clothes.

Father told the man they had not yet eaten their evening meal and for him to come in the tent and rest and mother would prepare supper and they would all eat together. To this the man replied he did not have time to stop and would prefer to have some food just to take along with him. Father asked him where he was going. He pointed to the southwest. Father then warned him not to go in that direction as it was barren desert and no water within sixty miles. To this the man replied, "I have traveled in the north, south, east and west, in heat and in cold, and I have no fear of suffering from thirst." Father then asked him his name, to which he replied, "They call me the Wandering Jew."

The stranger was given the things he asked for and father stepped into the tent. Mother said, "Don't let that man start over the desert this late in the day." So father hurried out to call him back to spend the night with them. The road stretched out for miles without obstruction, but the man could not be seen. A neighbor, Brother Fairbanks, had also seen the man as he approached my parents' tent, but had no conversation with him.

Father and mother always thought their visitor was John the Beloved, or one of the Three

Nephites, who had been promised by the Savior to tarry upon the earth until He returns again. *(Heart Throbs of the West, by Kate B. Carter. Daughters of Utah Pioneers. 1941. Vol. 3, pgs. 351-352.)*

Chapter Thirty-Nine

Did A Nephite Plow The Field?

David Whitmer

The fact is, it was just as though Joseph, Oliver and I were sitting just here on a log, when we were overshadowed by a light. It was not like the light of the sun nor like that of a fire but more glorious and beautiful. It extended away round us, I cannot tell how far, but in the midst of this light about as far off as he sits (pointing to John C. Whitmer, sitting a few feet from him), there appeared as it were, a table with many records or plates upon it, besides the plates of the Book of Mormon, also the Sword of Laban, the directors — i.e., the ball which Lehi had, and the Interpreters. I saw them just as plain as I see this bed (striking the bed beside him with his hand), and I heard the voice of the Lord, as distinctly as I ever heard anything in my life, declaring that the records of the plates of the

Book of Mormon were translated by the gift and power of God."

Orson Pratt: Did you see the Angel at this time?

David Whitmer: Yes; he stood before us. Our testimony as recorded in the Book of Mormon is strictly and absolutely true, just as it is there written. Before I knew Joseph, I had heard about him and the plates from persons who declared they knew he had them, and swore they would get them from him. When Oliver Cowdery went to Pennsylvania, he promised to write me what he should learn about these matters, which he did. He wrote me that Joseph had told him Oliver's secret thoughts, and all he had meditated about going to see him, which no man on earth knew, as he supposed, but himself, and so he stopped to write for Joseph.

Soon after this, Joseph sent for me, (David Whitmer) to come to Harmony to get him and Oliver and bring them to my father's house. I did not know what to do, I was pressed with my work. I had some 20 acres to plow, so I concluded I would finish plowing and then go. I got up one morning to go to work as usual, and on going to the field, found between five and seven acres of my ground had been plowed during the night.

I don't know who did it; but it was done just

as I would have done it myself, and the plow was left standing in the furrow.

This enabled me to start sooner. When I arrived at Harmony, Joseph and Oliver were coming toward me, and met me some distance from the house. Oliver told me that Joseph had informed him when I started from home, where I had stopped the first night, etc., and that I would be there that day before dinner, and this was why they had come out to meet me; all of which was exactly as Joseph had told Oliver, at which I was greatly astonished. When I was returning to Fayette, with Joseph and Oliver, all of us riding in the wagon, Oliver and I had an old fashioned wooden spring seat and Joseph behind us, while traveling along in a clear open place, a very pleasant, nice-looking old man suddenly appeared by the side of our wagon and saluted us with, "good morning, it is very warm," at the same time wiping his face or forehead with his hand. We returned the salutation, and, by a sign from Joseph, I invited him to ride if he was going our way. But he said very pleasantly, "No, I am going to Cumorah." This name was something new to me, I did not know what Cumorah meant. We all gazed at him and at each other, and as I looked around inquiringly of Joseph, the old man instantly disappeared, so that I did not see him again.

Joseph F. Smith: Did you notice his appearance?

David Whitmer: I should think I did. He was, I should think, about 5 feet 8 or 9 inches tall and heavy set, about such a man as James Vancleave there, but heavier; his face was as large, he was dressed in a suit of brown woolen clothes, his hair and beard were white, like Brother Pratt's, but his beard was not so heavy. I also remember that he had on his back a sort of knapsack with something in, shaped like a book. It was the messenger who had the plates, who had taken them from Joseph just prior to our starting from Harmony. Soon after our arrival home, I saw something which led me to the belief that the plates were placed or concealed in my father's barn. I frankly asked Joseph if my supposition was right, and he told me it was. *(Millennial Star, Vol. 40:772-773. 1878.)*

Chapter Forty

Famishing On An American Desert

Elizabeth J. Barney
J. Orson Barney

On the 8th day of December, 1895, my husband and I left Mexico enroute to St. George, Utah, for the purpose of performing temple work. We arrived at Ohajaca, Mexico, on the night of the 24th of December. At this place we were invited by friends to be their guests on Christmas day, but we were anxious to be on our way, so instead of spending Christmas day with our friends, we spent Christmas eve with them, staying up until the wee small hours of the morning, and on the morning of the twenty-fifth (Christmas day) we started for Mesa City, Arizona, arriving there the latter part of January, 1896, where my first child was born — a girl — April 28, 1896 being its natal day.

We left Mesa on the 8th day of June, 1896, in

company with mother, (Eliza M. R. Prows) and her four children — Lodeskey Prows, father's first wife, and two orphan children — Parley and Perry Miller, grandchildren of Lodeskey's. Also with us were Brother Bigelow, his daughter and son and his son's wife and their two children, and my husband, (Orson Barney) and I.

After traveling some time, we were anxious to get to a place called at that time "the Hole in the Rocks," a watering place on the desert which was located many miles from other watering places. On arriving at this place, it was found that there was very little water to be had. My husband said: "We will have to go on but will fill the five gallon keg for drinking purposes, and one bucket each for the horses," which we did. "We will have to travel tonight while it is cool as it will be forty miles before we can get more water." We traveled until a late hour that night and pitched camp. We got up the next morning just at the break of day and traveled until about nine o'clock, and then prepared something to eat. Every one was famished for want of water. The horses were so thirsty that they frothed at the mouth. The little children cried for water. We had to place pebbles in the children's mouths and have them drink but a swallow of water at a time.

We started on after partaking of the meal just

prepared, but had not gone but a few miles when the horses got so bad for the want of water that it was necessary to give them a half a bucket of water each. At first a little water was placed in the bottom of the bucket, but they were so thirsty that it was a great effort to get their heads from the bucket. A small baby became so sick that it had convulsions. It was administered to by my husband and Brother Bigelow and it revived as soon as they took their hands off its head.

We started on again, but had not gone over five or ten miles when, all of a sudden, a man was seen in the road ahead not over three hundred feet. Upon arriving at our side my husband stopped the team and inquired of the stranger where we could find water, stating to the stranger that the horses and all needed water so badly. At this time night was fast approaching. The stranger replied: "Yes, do you see that clump of green on that mountain?" (pointing to a green spot on a mountain some two miles distance). My husband said, "Yes." Continuing, the stranger said: "You drive just as close to it as you can but you will not be able to get very close to it. Make camp for the night at that place, for you will not be able to get any more water for forty miles. You must take every available utensil you have and fill it. Fill all your vessels." (In our wagon we had one forty-gallon barrel on one side and a twenty-five gallon barrel on the other and one five-gallon keg, and Brother Bigelow had the same kind and number of containers). "It may not be deep enough to put a bucket in but take something to dip the spring out."

When we arrived there, we found the prettiest spring I have ever seen, the water bubbling up, cool and delightfully refreshing. The men dug it out so that a bucket could be used in dipping the water to the barrels and kegs which were all filled. The stranger also said before leaving us: "Be sure and water your horses in the morning before you leave and give them all they can drink."

My husband stated to the stranger: "You had better not go on; there isn't a drop of water, not even in 'The Hole in the Rocks' water place. I have been over the road before," but the stranger replied: "I must be going." Saying this he raised his cap and walked briskly away, passing our wagon by the side of which this conversation had taken place, and then he passed Brother Bigelow's wagon. My husband looked backward to see the stranger pass Brother Bigelow's wagon, and then handed me the lines and he stood up on the spring seat so that he could get a good view of the stranger, but he could not see him. When he could not see him, we stopped our team and Brother Bigelow did the same. My husband got off the wagon and walked past the next wagon but there was no sign of the stranger.

When we arrived at St. George, we found the temple closed for the summer, so we went on to Kanosh, our birth place and home town, but later we went to Manti and did our temple work.

My husband and I both certify to the absolute truthfulness of this narrative, which we will remember as long as mortality shall last with us.

Signed: Elizabeth J. Barney
J. Orson Barney
Dated at Manti, Utah,
This 7th day of July, 1940.

Signatures Witnessed By:
Wm. N. Stevens
Randlett, Utah

(Assorted Gems of Priceless Value, N. B. Lundwall. 1944. pgs. 26-28.)

Chapter Forty-One

The Three Prophets

James H. McClintock

President Brigham Young kept the Hopi Indians in mind and in 1859 he sent Jacob Hamblin on a second trip to the Indians, with a company that consisted of Marion J. Shelton, Thales Haskell, Taylor Crosby, Benjamin Knell, Ira Hatch, and John Wm. Young. They reached the Hopi Indian villages November 6, talked with the Indians three days and then left the work of possible conversion on the shoulders of Shelton and Haskell, who returned to Santa Clara (Utah) the next spring. The Indians were kind, but unbelieving, and "could make no move until the reappearance of the Three Prophets who led their fathers to that land and told them to remain in those rocks until they should come again and tell them what to do." *(Mormon Settlement in Arizona, by James H. McClintock. University of Arizona Press. 1921. pgs. 65-66.)*

Chapter Forty-Two

An Indian Vision

G. W. Hill

In a former article I gave an account of my first day's work at baptizing the Indians on Bear River, after they had applied to me so many times to do so. I then promised to give the readers of the *Instructor* something more on the Indian question, and I shall now tell the reason those Lamanites were impelled to ask for baptism.

Four years ago last summer some of those Indians were encamped on the south side of Salt Lake, west of Skull Valley, when one day three strange men came into the lodge of the chief, whose name was Ech-up-wy, and after seating themselves commenced talking to him on religious matters. This seemed so strange to him that he turned and scrutinized them closely. The visitors were evidently Indians, as they had the Indian complexion. One of them was a very large, broad shouldered man, quite good looking; the other two were rather below the medium size. The large one was spokesman. They told him that the "Mormons" God was the true God, and that He and the Indians' Father were one; that he must go to the "Mormons" and they would tell him what to do, and that he must do it; that he must be baptized, with all his Indians; that the time was at hand for the Indians to gather, and stop their Indian life, and learn to cultivate the earth and build houses, and live in them. They then said to him "Look!" He turned his head, and, although he was sitting in his lodge, he saw all this northern country about Bear River and Malad. He saw small farms all over it with grain growing very finely, and small houses dotted here and there all over the land. He saw also that these were Indians' houses, and that there were a great many Indians at work, and apparently feeling first rate. He noticed also a few white men there showing the Indians how to work, one of whom he recognized as myself. What seemed more strange than anything else was that he could see down the canyons on both sides of the mountains, as he might do if he occupied a position in the air above them. After viewing this scene for some time, he turned his eyes in another direction, but not being satisfied he looked around to see more of it, when, to his surprise there was nothing visible before him but the bare side of the lodge. The visitors then told him that when he got his house built and got to living in it, they would come again to see him; they also said something he did not understand, when he turned to ask them an explanation, but, lo! they were gone. His buffalo robes were lying just as they had been, but no visitors were there.

The Indians immediately broke camp and came after me, and wanted me to baptize them, saying that their women and children wanted to be baptized as well as the men, and that it was not good for them to come to Ogden to have the ordinance attended to. They kept importuning for baptism, coming after me as often as once in every week or fortnight until the following spring, when I went and did my first day's work.

Ech-up-wy did not tell me at the first about this vision, nor in fact, anyone else; nor could he be made to believe that the places where they are now located was the proper place for them to make farms, although President Young directed that they should locate there, until, when work on the irrigating canal was commenced, he viewed from an eminence the very scene that was shown him in his vision. After that he was satisfied that he was at work in the right place, and told me of his vision, and the reason for demanding baptism.

As to whom the men were who visited Ech-up-wy, the readers can form their own conjecture; but one thing I can say, he has tried as hard to carry out the instructions given him as any man I ever saw. He now has got his house built, as have quite a number of others, and they feel like getting up out of the dirt. *(Juvenile Instructor, Vol. 12:11.)*

Chapter Forty-Three

Her Zion

John Samuel Hanks

Sarah Ann Morgan Edwards, wife of David Edwards, and the fifteenth child in a family of seventeen, was born January 14, 1819, in Merthyr Tydfil, South Wales. She was a convert to the "Mormon Church" by the missionaries of the Church in Wales.

For ten years the Edwards family contributed faithfully to the Emigration Fund of the Church, always with the hope that their selection to emigrate would soon be made. After ten years, Sarah requested of her husband that she be made his cashier, as she felt that in that manner they would soon be able to accumulate sufficient funds to pay their own passage to "Zion." At the end of a year David Edwards, Sarah's husband, died in one of the terrible epidemics of typhus fever of that time. His last request was, "Sarah, take the children to Zion."

A few months after my grandfather's death, my grandmother, together with her five children, left Wales for America with just enough money to pay their transportation to Salt Lake City. They arrived in the Valley in October of 1864. They were instructed by the authorities of the Church, after a three weeks rest in Salt Lake City, to proceed to southern Utah to make their future home. They therefore settled in Paragonah, Iron County, Utah.

In dire poverty, Sarah Ann Morgan Edwards endeavored to make a meager living for her little family; many times doing washing for people from door to door, many times barefooted. During their first winter in Paragonah, Sarah and her five little ones built for themselves a one-room log home. The furniture was of that home-made Pioneer type prevalent at that time, but was supplemented only by a few articles they had brought across the ocean and the plains. Among those pieces was a chest from Wales, which is kept in the family to this day.

Then one fine spring morning in that spring of 1865, Sarah Ann was sitting in front of her fireplace alone. This was about eleven o'clock in the morning. She was poorly clad, hungry, ill, and for the first time in her long struggle she was offering up a silent prayer of thankfulness that her husband had not lived to experience such hardship. At the close of the prayer she heard distinctly a knock at her door. She arose, opened the door, and there stood a tall, slender man, whose face was covered with a long, black beard. His countenance was serious, but very kindly, and he was dressed in the rough, home-made clothing of the Pioneers of that period. Grandmother invited him in and as he stepped inside the door, he said, "You did well, my daughter, to bring your five children to Zion." Sarah Ann turned to get a chair for her visitor, but when she turned again to the door he was gone.

In her surprise, she stepped to the door, looked down the street, but she could not find him, and never did she see her strange visitor again. She always contended that the mysterious man was one of the Three Nephites who roam the world until the coming of Christ.

Sarah Ann died November 7, 1901, at the age of 82 years. To the end of life she held a strong testimony of the faith, and though her last twelve years were spent in total blindness, she always retained a healthful attitude about life and the paths down which she had traveled. *(Heart Throbs of the West, by Kate B. Carter. Daughters of Utah Pioneers. 1941. Vol. 3, pg. 350.)*

Chapter Forty-Four

A Mysterious Preacher

Franklin Spencer

[The following letter, the writer of which is a missionary in the Southern States Mission, America, appeared in the Deseret News of May 17th: Shady Grove, Hickman Co., May 6th, 1880.]

Editors Deseret News;

In the month of April, 1878, one Robert Edge, a preacher of the Gospel after the apostolic order, came to and near Lexington, Henderson Co., Tennessee, and commenced warning the people of the judgements of God that will shortly come upon them for their wickedness. Spoke very lengthily upon the fulfillment of prophecy that was uttered by ancient prophets, and thoroughly proving the falling away and apostasy of the primitive Church; the killing of the Saints by Pagan Rome; the rise and progress of the Romish Church, as being mystery, Babylon, and

162

all her daughters and grand-daughters being under direct inspiration of Lucifer, the son of the morning; and all secret societies are institutions of men, and are an abomination in the sight of the Lord.

He dwelt very lightly on the principle of baptism, but extensively on the laying on of hands for the gift of the Holy Ghost; that the apostolic church was again restored on the earth, with prophets and apostles, baptism for the remission of sins, laying on of hands for the gift of the Holy Ghost, with signs following them that believe. By his administration four remarkable cases of healing occurred.

He positively refused money for his preaching. In the meantime the people became very curious to know who he was and what church he belonged to. Being asked if baptism is essential for salvation, he said it was a true principle, but the people did not understand it. Being asked if he had authority to baptize, said if he had not, there were many on the earth who did have. Being asked if there was an apostolic church on the earth, said there was, with many members. Being asked where it was, said it was in the United States, but avoided giving any further information.

After having delivered a series of sermons, he called upon all to come out of Mystery Babylon, forsake manmade institutions, and follow Christ in accordance with the apostolic order.

Sixty-three then agreed to follow him as he followed Christ. He then proceeded to organize them in a *brotherly love order*, after the apostolic order, by laying on hands and blessing them, and by requesting them to fast three days, and by instructing them not to marry outside of said order, saluting each other with the holy kiss, and if they would be honest, faithful and prayerful, the Lord would guide them by His Spirit in all things they should do to be saved; that there was more he would like to inform them upon, but persecution was rising, and he would shortly have to leave them; that if persecution arose so they had to leave, for them to go west of the Rocky Mountains for safety.

A lively persecution shortly arose, charging him to be a "Mormon" preacher, which he did not deny nor sanction, but his followers did deny that he or they were "Mormons."

Nineteen of the number fulfilled the requirements of the order of brotherly love, have withstood two years' persecution, more or less, and in the absence of their beloved preacher they have held weekly meetings.

In the fall of 1879, their attention was called to an interview between O. J. Hollister, a United

States official, and President John Taylor.

They then wrote to the county clerk of Salt Lake County for information, who kindly forwarded a "Voice of Warning," and a list of Church works, by which they sent for a full list of Church works, *Deseret News and Millennial Star.*

They wrote a letter of enquiry to President Morgan, who forwarded the same to me, which was promptly answered, and in reply to which James H. Scott and S. Reed came to Cane Creek, Lewis County, a distance of fifty miles, and after hearing our views of the Gospel, which coincided with the teaching of Mr. Edge, they were baptized and confirmed by Brother Hyrum Belnap and myself, and returned home rejoicing that they had thus far followed the promptings of the Spirit of the Lord.

Since Brother Argyle left me in charge of this Mission, Dec. 17th, 1879, eleven members have been added to the Church. Elders Carver, Belnap and Hunsaker are active in their mission and enjoying the same. *(Millennial Star, Vol. 42:399.)*

Chapter Forty-Five

Diamond In The Cave

A Danish-Norwegian periodical published in Utah (1884) ran a story from South America about a Nephite experience there:

"The letter, which was received in Santos, S. Paulo (Brazil), from a son who lives in Batataes, contains the following account: 'A man who guards cattle on the prairie about 25 miles from here came to a rock in which he found an opening. He entered it and instantly found himself in an extraordinary cave. Near its bottom something shone which resembled a diamond. At the same moment he heard lovely music, but taken by fright, he fled in haste. As a result of the herdsman's story many people betook themselves to the cave with the intention of draining the water of the pond to secure the diamond; and after some labor they succeeded in lowering the water to a point where it was clearly seen, but then they found a door in the side of the rock wall which they opened. There upon they saw a dark passageway, but because at the same time they beheld a man in blue clothing no one dared to enter. In the morning (18 March) about 20 well-weaponed men intend to go to the place. I am taking part in the expedition."

"The result of the expedition is related in the following letter, dated Batataes, 1 April, 1867: 'After a long day's ride we came to the vicinity of the rock, where the entrance was soon found. We hastily took the saddles off our mules, which we let loose in the grass while we sat down to eat and talk together around the campfire. We passed the time in interesting conversation and narration of stories until the moon rose, when we betook ourselves to the great rock nearby, in which our guide at once pointed out the cave's entrance; it was small and close to the earth. We found the opening to the other cave, which was much larger than the first, and our light was lost in its immensity. After we had gone about 50 "Brakaer" the passageway suddenly opened upon a little cave which resembled a room lighted by something which seemed like a gigantic diamond, whose light showed us a little stone table around which on rock stools sat three middle-aged men with noble features, dressed in long blue habits, which were bound fast around the wearer's body with a white belt which glittered with gold stars and with great blood-red carbuncles. These remarkable personages seemed apparently deeply preoccupied with the contents of a scroll which lay unrolled before them. We reflected whether or not to speak to them, because although they apparently were living beings, there was something striking in their appearance, that we were filled with awe and wonder. At last Jose Luiz de Paula Silva could no longer resist the temptation to draw near the table to examine the beautiful treasure which lay in the middle of the table. Instantly and simultaneously the three readers raised their heads and — but I cannot say what actually took place there. It seems to me as if a dreadful and irresistible wind enveloped us and sped us forward. I do not remember more. When I returned to consciousness I found myself and my comrades lying on the ground where we had eaten our evening meal; we were unhurt but entirely confused in mind. The following morning we searched the neighborhood again. The great rock was still there, but the entrance to the cave had disappeared.

That these Three Nephite apostles are still found on earth there can be no doubt. *(Der Tre Nephiter, Morgenstjernen. Translated by William Mulder. January 15, 1884. Vol. 3, No. 2, pg. 24.)*

Chapter Forty-Six

The Helping Hand

W. L. Olsten

In the early settlement of Emery County, Utah, three families left Ephraim, Utah, to settle there. Mr. W. L. Olsten and his wife related the following:

"On their way down Huntington Canyon, as they were traveling along a narrow rough dugway, they came to a place where there had been a huge slide of shale and rock that had covered the road. The shale was loose, the ledge below was hundreds of feet straight up and down, as well as the ledge on the other side was high and steep. They stopped, and as they were figuring how they would manage the situation, because they could not turn back, a man came along with a satchel in his hand. He was neatly dressed, but dusty and travel-worn. He stopped and in a second or two said: 'I see that you are in a very dangerous place and you need help. One more man will make it safer, so I'll stay and help you.' He managed the situation. He told the man who was on lead with his team to go over the road first, the others to stay where they were until the first wagon was safely located on the dugway beyond the rock and shale. He said that he would walk along the lower side and hold the wagon in place. This he did. After the three outfits, with the women and children, were all helped to their place of safety, as they were thanking the stranger for his wonderful help, he walked a few steps away from the group and suddenly disappeared. They always felt that this man was one of the Three Nephites." *(Heart Throbs of the West, by Kate B. Carter. Daughters of Utah Pioneers. 1941. Vol. 3, pgs. 358-359.)*

Chapter Forty-Seven

A Wonderful Testimony

Maude May Babcock

During the summer of 1900, Maude May Babcock and a friend, Carrie Helen Lamson, were spending their vacation at Brighton. On one of their trips exploring the wonders of Brighton, she relates the following experience:

"We discussed our plan with those around camp and were told it was feasible. So a week later we started out on horseback. We were directed to take a shorter trail above Dog Lake to Lake Catherine, and to take that divide rather than the longer way over the Alta pass by the Twin Lakes. It is a trail I now know well, but it was new to me then. We reached, as we thought, the trail near a deserted mine camp over Dog Lake about seven o'clock in the morning, but soon could get no farther, nor get back without crossing a crevice filled with shale. I tried to force my horse across, but when the shale began to slide, he would not move. Miss Lamson's horse would not make the attempt, and they were farther down the side of the mountain than I was. Seeing that both my horse and I were in danger of sliding down the mountain a thousand or more feet, I dismounted as carefully as I could, in fear of my own life and that of my horse. I climbed slowly and carefully around the shale bed up to the top of the mountain to look for help, hoping that I might see some stray prospector. But no; although the top was like a lawn, sloping in every direction, no one was in sight. Not a living thing to be seen; only the grandeur of the mountains spread before me in the stillness of the early morning. Disappointed, I cautiously climbed over the jagged peak above my horse, and half holding to a small bush with my hands, and half holding by my feet in that sliding shale, I reached down to my horse, almost under me, and touched him with a small willow, trying to coax him across the shale. He would not move. At this crucial moment, fearing the horse would any moment slide down the mountain and I would be dashed to death after him if the shale began to move, I prayed to Heavenly Father for help. As I raised my head a voice above me said, 'How did you come here, my daughter?' I jabbered in my relief and excitement, trying to explain our predicament, and before my explanation was finished I was standing on the top, with Miss Lamson and both our

horses in a circle facing the stranger. We had no
recollection of how we or the horses got there. The
man had a gray Vandyke beard, a cap on his head,
and was dressed in very new blue overalls. He was
very clean and I was surprised to notice his white
hands as if unused to manual labor. He addressed me
as 'My Daughter,' but although Miss Lamson asked
him several questions, he directed his answers always
to me instead of her. I inquired about the road and
the way and he said 'Go right on, my daughter, the
way you are going, and you will be all right.' While
talking to him, unconsciously, we got on our horses.
Before we had gone twenty feet, it came to me I had
failed to thank the man who had saved our lives. I
turned to atone for my neglect and ingratitude, but
although we could see at least a mile in every
direction, the stranger had vanished. We seemed to
have been in a daze from the wonder and marvel of
our experience, which had seemed perfectly natural,
when it rushed over me and as inspired, I said, "He
was one of the Three Nephites."

"Miss Lamson was not in the Church. She did
not even believe in God. In our discussions and
arguments and during our readings of Matthew
Arnold and Walter Pater, I had explained the Gospel
restored, but she could not understand me, nor was
she at all interested. She asked who was a Nephite?
And as we rode along that early morning, with the

spirit of the stranger with us, I explained the Book of Mormon, and told how the Savior, when visiting His people on the American Continent, had granted Three Nephite Apostles the blessing bestowed upon John the Beloved, to tarry and preach the Gospel until He should come again." During the next three days, I explained the principles of the Gospel — indeed, we talked of nothing else. As I was talking of the stranger, I suddenly was aware of peculiar hobnail footprints pointing toward us on the trail. We met the stranger about seven o'clock in the morning and we followed the foot prints always coming to meet us, until we reached the American Fork Canyon, after one o'clock that afternoon. Whenever I thought I could make a short cut, I would be forced to come back to the footprints, for the way would be impassable. When we came down the mountain into the canyon, we met some miners, the first persons we had seen since the stranger left us. They advised us not to go through the South Fork into the North Fork of the Provo, because of deep snow, but to go instead through Deer Creek into Provo Canyon. I should have trusted my stranger, for we found the journey long and tiresome and did not reach camp until after midnight. We lost the footprints when we left American Fork Canyon. I have always believed we would have found the way passable, and that the foot prints would have led us over the mountain, and we would have seen the glacier behind Timpanogos, which we had planned to see.

Near us, nestling in the very tops of the mountain range, we could count thirteen lakes, while to the east, range upon range of blue mountains, like great billows of the ocean, seemed to roll on and on into space. With this view before us, and with the spirit of adventure within us, I then made a plan to go farther and make a two days' trip over the trail we had come and on into American Fork Canyon, through its South Fork into Provo Canyon, and to spend a night at the South Fork of the Provo. The second day we could go up the canyon to Midway and the Hot Pots, and over the mountains back to Brighton.

The next day's journey over the mountains back to Brighton was spent with joy, talking of the things of the Gospel, and God's wonderful manifestations to his children in these last days. Our friends welcomed us, as the whole camp were ready to take up a hunt for us, fearing we were lost in the mountains.

The spirit, influence and testimony of these three days in the mountains has remained with me all these years, to strengthen my faith, the knowledge of God, His works, and conviction that God answers prayer. Miss Lamson was so affected by our experience, that there came to her a testimony that we have a Heavenly Father, that He lives and answers individual prayer. She soon after received a testimony of the Gospel and joined the church. *(Juvenile Instructor, Nov. 1921. Vol. 56:584-587.)*

Chapter Forty-Eight

The Food Was Restored

A woman who was living near the Brigham Young University housed two students who did odd jobs for board. In the morning, after they had left for school, a heavy snow began to fall and had accumulated to about six inches by noon, when the woman expected the boarders home for lunch. While she was preparing the meal, she heard a knock at the French doors, which were located on the side of her house and never used for entrance. She went to the doors and was confronted by a man who asked for something to eat. Inviting him in, she told him to sit down at the table, and while he ate she talked with him. When he had finished his meal, he thanked her, blessed her, and left, insisting on departing through the French doors as he had come. She closed the doors after him, turned to clear the table of dishes, and was astonished. There was his entire meal untouched — yet she had watched him eat it. The young boarders came dashing home with snow on their feet. While they wiped their shoes, the woman reflected that there had been no snow on the stranger's shoes. Rushing to the French doors, she threw them wide and looked across the snow. It was smooth and untouched. No footprints were visible. *(Anonymous manuscript in the archives of the Utah Humanities Research Foundation.)*

Chapter Forty-Nine

Our Strange Visitor

Mesach S. Williams

A peculiar incident is related by Brother Mesach S. Williams, of Samaria, as having occurred while he was living in Willard City, in the Spring of 1856.

It was at the time of scarcity, when bread-stuff was hard to obtain. We give it to our readers, in substance, as it was presented to us by Brother Williams.

On one particular day of that year, Brother Williams' family had barely enough bread for dinner. He had just then concluded to go out (as many others did at that time) to hunt segos, and requested his wife to give him a sack to put them in. His wife, somewhat overcome by the gloomy prospect before them, was in tears. Brother Williams encouraged her as much as possible and was about to start out upon his errand when a knock was heard at the door. He opened it and an old gentleman presented himself. His hair and beard were as white as snow, and he appeared to be very old, but, nevertheless, fresh and active. His dress was ragged in the extreme, but scrupulously clean. He had on a very nice white shirt and his coat resembled what was conjectured by Brother Williams to have once been a white blanket.

Upon invitation he came in and sat down near Brother Williams, at the same time remarking that times were very bad. He said:

"Brother, there is enough bread-stuff in the Territory to supply this people for three years, if properly distributed; but it is in the hands of the rich and they, it seems, will not impart of their substance unto the poor. Notwithstanding all this, however, it is the work of the living God."

He then asked if they had any bread in the house. Brother Williams told him they had just about enough for dinner; but that he was welcome to a portion of it. He was given an equal share of the bread, which he put in his bosom, between his shirt and garments, with the remark:

"You will live to see a great many changes occur among this people; but always bear in mind that this is the work of the Lord."

He asked Sister Williams if she had a needle and thread she could lend him a few minutes. His request was complied with and he commenced sewing something on the sleeve of his coat. Although crediting himself with the possession of keen sight, Brother Williams says he failed to discover what it was that the old gentleman was sewing to his sleeve.

At this juncture it may be said that the only thread they were in possession of at that time was what they themselves had made from flax, which we may imagine was not very fine.

After having used it for some time, he returned the needle and walked towards the door. Stopping in the doorway, he raised his right hand and said:

"I tell you, in the name of Israel's God, you will never see the want of bread; no, never!"

He walked out and closed the door. Brother Williams followed as soon as possible, but, to his surprise, on getting outside the old gentleman was not in sight. He had disappeared in the course of two or three seconds and could not now be seen anywhere. This seemed to confirm a belief that Sister Williams had entertained while the old gentlemen was in the house, that he was not a mortal being.

Brother Williams proceeded to carry out his

intentions in regard to obtaining some segos to eat, when the first person whom he met was Bishop Charles Hubbard, who enquired as to whether or not Brother Williams had any bread-stuff. He told him they had scarcely any in the house. The Bishop said:

"I was thinking of you a few moments ago, wondering if you had anything to eat. I have thirty pounds of flour in a sack for you; go and get it, and when that is finished come and get some more."

Brother Williams took the flour with a thankful heart and proceeded towards his home. When passing the house of a Brother Harding, that gentleman called out to him and said he had a bushel of wheat in the house which had been left there for him. Brother Williams was elated with his success and pursued his way joyfully, when he was met by Bishop George Ward, who told him he had been thinking of his circumstances, and that he had four bushels of wheat for him, which he could pay for in labor. This Brother Williams was very thankful to do.

On his reaching home, Sister Williams was still in tears. She could scarcely believe him when he told her he had thirty pounds of flour, and she was not thoroughly satisfied until he had opened the sack and showed it to her. She said that this was really a fulfillment of the words of the old gentleman who had so lately visited them. And further, Brother

Williams says he has never since been without plenty of bread.

In a subsequent conversation with Patriarch John Young upon this matter, Brother Williams says he was told by him that the old gentleman spoken of was one of the Three Nephites that were to tarry upon the earth. Brother Williams also states this to be his firm belief. At all events it was a peculiar circumstance; and the incidents connected with it seem to bear the marks of a power that is infinitely greater than that of man.

Whenever strangers appear at our doors requesting food, we should extend our hospitality to them; for, although they may not be persons of the same description as the subject of this sketch, we know not what pain and suffering we, in our acts of kindness, may relieve, or what sorrow and remorse would result in a refusal on our part to grant them food or shelter, which they may sorely need. *(Juvenile Instructor. 1886. Vol. 21, pg. 103.)*

Chapter Fifty

The White Bread On The White Cloth

Norma Schofield

John and Isabella lived in a one-room home south of Thirty-ninth South on West Temple, Salt Lake City. Their first child, John Price, Jr., was just an infant and was very, very sick, and nothing they had done had helped. They had prayed and prayed for help, but his condition continued to grow worse. One night after they had retired and the room was still lighted by the fire from the fireplace, there came a knock on the door. Grandpa Price opened the door, and there stood a stranger, a fine looking man dressed in a gray suit. He asked for shelter for the night. Great-grandfather Price told him that they had only one room and that there were no extra beds, but the stranger said that he'd be content if he could sit by the fire and keep warm for the night.

And so he was invited in.

As the stranger settled himself by the fire, the child, who had not rested well for days, sank into a peaceful sleep. Grandpa had determined to stay awake to watch the man, but he himself seemed unable to stay awake. During the night Grandma awoke with a start, worried because she had fallen asleep with her sick child there. Then she saw this stranger sitting at the table, and the table was covered with a cloth so brilliantly white that she could hardly look at it. She nudged Grandpa, and they watched him eat bread of the same brilliant white. As they looked, they knew that he must be a heavenly being, and they said nothing. The next morning when they arose, they offered the stranger breakfast, but he refused.

The home in which they lived was surrounded by bare ploughed ground, without even a tree near. And Grandpa walked out of the house with the man, and as they turned the corner he started to say something to the stranger, and the man had disappeared entirely. As he went back into the house, Grandma Price met him and told him that the baby was absolutely well and playing in the crib. They knew that this man had been sent in answer to their prayers, and believed him to be one of the Three Nephites.

Q: They had no idea where the bread might have come from?

A: No, they had no idea. They had no bread, of course, of that hue in their home. Nor the cloth. The cloth didn't belong to them at all. *(The Three Nephites, by Hector Haight Lee. The University of New Mexico. 1949. pgs. 137-138.)*

Chapter Fifty-One

The Pillar Of Prophecy

Charles F. Steele

The predictions of the servants of the Lord never fail, although at the time of their utterance the fulfillment, in the eyes of men, may appear utterly impossible. This truth is attested by a silent witness which stands on the corner of Broad and Fifth streets of Augusta, Georgia. It is locally known as the Pillar of Prophecy.

An interesting story is attached to this old landmark, and it is often recalled from the dusty recesses of memory to impress one with the fundamental truth that God lives and never forgets the utterance of His authorized servants.

The Pillar of Prophecy is a white, concrete shaft, perhaps twelve feet in height. It stands in the center of the sidewalk, the pavement having been laid around it, leaving the Pillar undisturbed. This fact is very significant in that Broad Street is the principal thoroughfare of the city, and space is, therefore, valuable. The significance becomes plain when the story of the Pillar is told.

It is a story that dates back more than thirty years, when Augusta was first catching the glimpse of her present greatness, when she was undergoing the process of transition from a city of the Old South to one of the New. The incident was known then to Augustans, first hand, the old-timers handing it down to their posterity, as a thing worth remembering.

And now for the story. There appeared on the streets of Augusta about thirty years ago a stranger. He was a man of mystery. No one knew whence he came, nor whither he departed. He was a preacher who, like the prophets of old, cried repentance unto the city. He is described as a man of average height, with hair of pure white and neatly trimmed, stately in appearance, and possessing a voice clear and pleasing, yet incisive, even to the piercing of the human heart.

This unknown evangelist usually spoke in the Market Place. This was composed of two large sheds, extending about one hundred feet across the street (the street is one hundred and eighty feet from curb to curb), and about two hundred feet long. The sheds were supported by pillars. One shed was known as the "Upper Market," the other the "Lower Market." Here the people of the city gathered each morning to purchase their daily supply of produce from the farmers coming in from the surrounding country.

A remarkable prophecy was made by the Preacher. He predicted that the "Lower Market" would be destroyed by a storm, but that the southwest corner post would remain as a testimony to the people that he was a prophet of God, and that his warning message was true. He further solemnly averred that if anyone attempted to move the Pillar that person would die.

Shortly after the utterance of this strange prophecy, a devastating electrical storm swept over the city of Augusta, destroying the "Lower Market" but leaving, as the Prophet had said, the south-west pillar.

The Pillar of Prophecy still stands. No one has ventured to move it. Neither man nor woman exhibit any willingness to take the risk. The Pillar also survived the fury of the great fire of 1916, which practically obliterated the business district of Augusta. The Pillar escaped unscathed, although buildings around it are still lying in ruins.

The mysterious Prophet was later entertained at the home of Mr. and Mrs. Mack Little, of

Groveland, Georgia, which is located about fifteen miles west of Augusta. In conversation with Mr. Little, the Prophet reiterated the direful prediction made on the streets of the city. The Little family still reside in Richmond county, and vouch for the truth of the story. They testify that the stranger never divulged his identity, and that he was never seen again.

Who was this Prophet? Old time Augustans believe him to be John the Baptist, or some other of the Biblical prophets. But Latter-day Saints are of the belief that the stranger may have been one of the Three Nephite apostles who were graciously permitted by the Christ to tarry on the earth until he should return in glory.

Said the risen Lord to the three apostles, discerning their desires: "Behold, I know your thoughts, and ye have desired the thing which John, my beloved, who was with me in my ministry, before that I was lifted up by the Jews, desired of me; therefore more blessed are ye, for ye shall never taste of death, but ye shall live to behold all the doings of the Father, unto the children of men, even until all things shall be fulfilled, according to the will of the Father, when I shall come in my glory, with the powers of heaven; and ye shall never endure the pains of death; but when I shall come in my glory, ye shall be changed in the twinkling of an eye from mortality to immortality: and then shall ye be blessed in the kingdom of my Father" (Book of Mormon, III Nephi 28:6-8).

Additional testimony that this prophet may have been one of the Three Nephite apostles was furnished the writer by Patriarch David F. Fawns, of Raymond, Canada. Elder Fawns fulfilled a mission in Georgia, over twenty years ago. On this mission much of his time was spent in Augusta. He testifies that while standing beside the Pillar, a personage approached and stood before him. Twice this manifestation appeared, and so vividly impressed was he that he can to this day minutely describe the person and his garb. His glorious, radiant countenance is one that will bless Elder Fawn's memory for ever, he declares.

The Pillar is an object of wonder and curiosity to the people of Augusta in general. To the Latter-day Saints it is especially significant, for it indicates to them that the three ancient American apostles are engaged in ministering among us as the Savior commissioned them to do, centuries ago. *(Improvement Era, Vol. 23:247-249.)*

Chapter Fifty-Two

My Experience

Thomas Palmer

Twenty-six years ago I had been seriously ill for several months. In April or May I went to the hospital with three abscesses on my lungs and stayed there for about ten days. I had been promised complete recovery by the Elders of the Church from the beginning of my illness.

After returning home, I did not regain my health as I was promised. The doctor said there was very little hope of complete recovery. I became very discouraged with the condition I was in, my family was really in need, my crops had been a complete failure, so I decided to ask the Lord why I had been deprived of the promises of the Priesthood.

I prayed, asking if there was anything standing in the way that I could overcome. As a direct answer to my prayer, in the night three personages visited me and stood at the foot of my bed and told me I would completely recover and before morning that which was on my lungs would slip on and I would regain my health and strength and would enjoy better health than I ever had. The three personages were about medium size, and had very mild, pleasing voices. I did not see from where they came or where they went, but I have enjoyed that blessing they promised me and at 81 years I enjoy perfect health and work on my farm each year.

There is no doubt in my mind but that these personages were the Three Nephites spoken of in the Book of Mormon, and were privileged to tarry on earth until the Savior comes. *(Heart Throbs of the West, by Kate B. Carter. Daughters of Utah Pioneers, 1941. Vol. 3, pgs. 354-355.)*

Chapter Fifty-Three

Catholic Girl and the Three Nephites

Mary Rinehart

This marvelous experience occurred when I was a young, sixteen year old girl. An experience which changed my life and eventually the lives of my future family.

My name is Mary Rinehart and I am sharing this wonderful event from my home in Las Vegas, Nevada. In the year 1947, I came down with a serious case of "double carbuncles" which turned into acute blood poisoning which in many instances is terminal. Carbuncles are very painful, infected and inflamed tissue openings beneath the skin which are more severe than a boil. I was very, very sick and allergic to the medication that I had been given for the carbuncles on my arm.

At this time I was living in Evanston, Indiana

and was a devout member of the Catholic Church. After being given the medication and returning home I had a threateningly adverse reaction and felt I would die. Suddenly, three men appeared before me and made me stand up even though I was very ill. These three were dressed differently than other people in Indiana; their hair and clothing was strange which made it all the more memorable to me. I thought that I was dreaming, but it was very real. The three gentlemen forced me to go to my Aunt Viola Nichols room where I collapsed to the floor in her doorway. They told me that my "mission" was not yet finished. This I remember, but did not fully understand.

I was rushed back to the hospital by ambulance in very critical condition; on the verge of dying. Had the three strangers in my home not appeared and compelled me to rise and go to my Aunt Vi, I surely would have expired. The doctors in the hospital emergency room said that if I had been any later arriving, that I certainly would have died. The three visitors literally saved my life. They appeared suddenly, and vanished just as quickly as they appeared. How they entered and left our home without Aunt Vi or anyone detecting them is a miracle beyond any explanation.

After my hospital recovery and upon regaining

my good health, I asked my Catholic priest, Father Brickner, for an explanation of this manifestation of three men to me and how they were able to detect my illness and save my life. He told me that it must have been my "guardian angels" who were watching over me.

In 1970, I left the Catholic Church and at that time was living with my husband in California. I lost all interest in religion and it was not until 1976 after looking for a more fulfilling faith, that a friend of mine said, "you're so upset, can I send the Mormon missionaries to you?"

The gospel of Jesus Christ, as taught by the Mormon missionaries, in Simi Valley, California seemed so familiar to me, and felt so right, that we were baptized and joined The Church of Jesus Christ of Latter-day Saints. After my husband and mother were baptized, I became heavily involved in family history and genealogy work and after my mother passed away, we retired and moved to Las Vegas.

The genealogy work has been tremendous! I have extracted over 5,000 new names which have been submitted, and I do a great deal of temple work here in our new temple. After receiving my Patriarchal Blessing and talking with other church leaders, and a special missionary friend, Elder Lane Clark, I suddenly realized that those three special men who saved my life 46 years ago were in fact, the Three Nephites! Their special missionary efforts in my behalf have not only benefited the living, but also the dead. I can see the Nephites today, as vivid as if it happened yesterday. *(Transcribed on December 29, 1992 by Douglas Beardall in personal interview as attested to by Mary Rinehart.)*

Chapter Fifty-Four

Preaching The Gospel In Many Lands

Hazel L. Shill

On the morning of the 19th of March, 1940, at about 7 o'clock, I was going out into the yard taking care of some of the duties of the household, and upon opening the door an elderly man stood about four feet from the kitchen door from which I had just come. His hair was not entirely gray but it had streaks of gray. He was about five feet eleven inches in height, was not especially heavy set, but weighing about one hundred sixty pounds. He wore a beard but no mustache, trimmed, and was tidily dressed with a dark suit. He wore a light gray overcoat of light weight. He looked very kind, his eyes were grayish blue, and he wore a light gray hat. Upon seeing him, he took off his hat and said: "Good morning, my dear, can you spare time to fix me a bit of breakfast." I at first thought I would say "no," but he looked so kind and clean that I said: "Sure, come in," both of us walking toward the kitchen door and he following me. I set a chair before him and invited him to sit down which he did, this being in the kitchen. I immediately started to fix breakfast for him. He sat and watched me and soon he said: "It has been many years since I have been in this part of the Lord's vineyard. I was amazed at the growth of Mesa." I made some reply which I do not now recall. He went on to ask: "Is the Church growing rapidly?" to which I answered "Yes, it is, especially here. My father came with the early pioneers and I can remember as a child there were such a few, but now there are ten wards in this Stake." He said: "My dear, your father was very fortunate to be called as one of the pioneers. I have been in Mexico for many years laboring in that branch of the Church." (It struck me at the time as peculiar when he called it a branch). "You will live to see the day when that part of the Lord's vineyard and this part will be as brothers. I visited with the Saints on the coast last week. The Lord is not pleased with His people there; they are living too fast. They let the real things of life slip behind while they take up the unimportant things. They are like most of the people now; they pray with their lips and have no faith in their hearts." Continuing he said: "The condition of the world is dreadful. In Germany there are many of the Lord's choice people, and in no other way could the gospel be spread only through this dreadful war."

All this was said while I was preparing the meal, after which I set it down before him. While he was eating I washed the morning dishes. I asked him if he would have anything else and he said: "Thank you, my dear." When I was fixing his breakfast I said: "Do you like your eggs poached hard or soft," to which he replied: "My dear, even as you have done it unto the least of these you have done it unto me." During the entire visit I felt a very serene, peaceful and quiet feeling. After finishing his breakfast, he arose, took his overcoat which he had put over a chair, and as he reached the door he turned and said: "You may not think much of this coming from me, but I promise you that through your faith, you nor yours shall never want."

Before going to the door I handed him his hat. He then said: "Good morning" and I replied "Good morning" and he was gone. All the while my son, Robert Shill, was in the adjoining room from the kitchen and after the stranger had left, he immediately came into the kitchen and said, "Mom, who was that man?" He was the queerest talking man I ever heard." To which I replied: "I don't know, son, but he dressed so well and looked so well kept to be asking for breakfast."

We both walked out of the house, not more than one minute from the time he left the kitchen door, going clear to the road which was about three hundred feet from the kitchen, but could see no one. He could not be seen in any direction, the road going straight for two miles in either direction. I have wondered and pondered about it so much and feel assured in my own heart and mind it was one of the Three Nephites. It would have taken at least a few minutes to go to the road and we went out immediately after he left.

This incident occurred in the settlement of Lehi, Maricopa County, Maricopa Stake, Arizona, on our twenty acre farm. The Latter-day Saint church is located about one thousand feet from our home and the school house about the same distance.

Signed the 7th day of April, 1940.
Signed: Hazel L. Shill
Signature witnessed by: N. B. Lundwall, Wm. F. Gollaher, Alice Gollaher (*Assorted Gems of Priceless Value, N. B. Lundwall. 1944. pgs. 22-24.*)

Chapter Fifty-Five

Was He One Of Them?

Mary Wells Whitney

Every reader of the Book of Mormon is familiar with the story of the Three Nephites, and the wonderful promise made to them by the Saviour that they should remain on earth superior to death, and bring souls to him; a promise similar to that given to the Apostle John (John 21:20-23; D.& C. 7).

There have been various instances of the fulfillment of the Saviour's promise to the Three Nephites in the experience of members of The Church of Jesus Christ of Latter-day Saints. One of special interest at the present time is a personal reminiscence of Sister Mary Wells Whitney, who is now connected with the European mission. Here it is, as related by Sister Whitney to the present writer:

"The incident happened many years ago, at our home in SaltLake City. My husband was away, and the only other members of the family in the house besides myself were three of our little boys. It was early spring and I was busy house-cleaning. Hearing the door bell ring, I went to the door, opened it, and there stood an elderly man, with white hair and beard, neatly dressed, straight as an arrow, and altogether respectable in appearance and respectful in manner. He asked me if I could help him. I told him I had no money, but if he needed food I would gladly give him some. He answered: "I would be very grateful."

"The unusual answer somewhat surprised me, but being very much occupied at the time, I paid but little attention. I showed him down into the kitchen, on the basement floor, spread what I had before him, and left him sitting at the table. The little boys were playing there at the time, and I told them to stay with the stranger and wait on him, while I returned to my work on the floor above."

"After a while I heard the clatter of feet running up the stairs; and here came the boys, all breathless and excited, the oldest exclaiming: 'Mama, I bet that was one of the Three Nephites.' 'What makes you think so?' I inquired. Here spoke up the second boy, who had had the toothache when the visitor arrived: 'I was holding my hand to my face, and he said, Son, what is troubling you? I said, I've got the toothache, and then he said, It will ache no more. And it stopped aching right then, and hasn't ached since.' The boys also told me that when the stranger departed, he said: 'Peace be unto you and your house.' They likewise related how they rushed out after him, and looked up and down the street, and through the back yard, but could not see him anywhere. My youngest son said: 'Mama, I even looked into the furnace room, and he wasn't there.'

"I do not think I am over-credulous in regard to such things, but the impression made upon my mind by that venerable stranger and his pleasing address, coupled with the excitement of the boys and their expressed conviction as to who he was, caused me to marvel. I have never been able to entirely banish the thought that possibly the boys were right." *(Millennial Star, editorial. Dec. 15, 1921.)*

Chapter Fifty-Six

Was It A Mirage?

Wilmer Bronson

I am here writing an account of a startling experience that came to my mother, my youngest brother, and to myself, and which was witnessed by all of us together.

Somewhere, deep in the profound mysteries of nature, as we come to understand them in our mortal state, or perhaps reposing in the infinite realms of truth, is the answer to what we saw.

I was in my sixteenth year, in the fall of 1894. I lived in Monticello, San Juan County. It was the custom of some of our townspeople to make a trip to Bluff, where fruit grew in abundance, in the fall of each year and purchase our fruit for canning. For this fruit we sometimes traded small grains which we grew in the higher altitude of Monticello. Mother had gone to Bluff with my father and youngest brother, who was eight years old, to dry and bottle fruit. She kept the boy with her, the two staying with my sister. Father returned and when mother was ready to come home, father sent me, with the team and wagon, to bring her home.

I well remember the Friday morning when we climbed aboard the wagon and started for home, because nearly all night Thursday the rain poured in torrents. The air was fresh and clean. The last words mother said to my sister, as the wagon began to roll, were: "Well, I would like to be here for conference tomorrow, but I guess I can't." In those days the quarterly conferences of the San Juan Stake of Zion were really events in our lives. They began on Saturday and ended the following Monday, with a dance or a drama.

We had climbed up the steep, winding road of the deep canyon, in which Bluff is situated, and looked out over the sandy plain stretching for miles in every direction. We were so glad to be alive on such a glorious morning. Some two or three hundred yards directly in front of us the road made a turn to the east and ran on the north side of a rather prominent sand dune, and then straightened out north again, in which direction we were traveling. Suddenly, in the bright morning sunlight, we saw the most splendid team of bay horses, with new harness, come trotting proudly from the opposite side of the sand dune, drawing behind them a glittering vehicle with red wheels and shining, black body. We were all awe-struck at the splendid sight. The vehicle was a two-seated one, with a man and a woman occupying each set. The women were dressed all in white and their clothing seemed very bright in the strong sunlight. The men wore the conventional dress of the day — white shirts, dark suits and high, silk hats. I noticed that the man who drove held his hands well out in front of him; the lines were tight and the horses seemed to be impatient to go faster as they leaned against the bits, and as the wheels turned around the sunlight was reflected from the spokes, so bright was the paint they bore. These details we all positively noted as we watched the team round the turn in the road and bear down straight upon us. We were by now coming close together, our outfit and theirs. Suddenly mother exclaimed: "O my gracious, I have to get this dirty apron off before we meet such fine people," and she quickly thrust her hands behind her to untie the apron she had been working in. My brother and I watched her; all our heads were for the second bowed and our eyes diverted from the oncoming vehicle, and when mother got her apron off and we all looked ahead again, the team, buggy , men and women had all disappeared completely. We expected to have to turn out for them in another thirty yards, but we were again alone on the wide desert. Mother became so frightened she trembled and my kid brother just kept saying: "Well, mamma, where have they gone to? Where are they? How could they go like that?"

By now we were well past the point where we should have met those people and when we examined the ground there was not a track of horse or vehicle to be seen anywhere. Around the sand dune we went, examining the road and the land on each side of us, but no marks of any kind were visible, and what made us more sure of our findings was the fact that the rainfall during the night before had obliterated every track of man or beast.

Mother was so frightened it was quite pitiful. I was dumb with wonder and a good many explanations were trying to force themselves into my reason as an answer to what we had seen. Mother had me walk out over the rising ground on each side of the road and see if I could get sight of any living thing. All I could see was what appeared to be a cow away to the east of us.

When we started on our way again, mother said: "Why what can it be? How could they get out of our sight when we saw them so plainly?" I answered that I guessed they weren't there or we would have seen their tracks. "Oh don't try to tell me I didn't see them," mother exclaimed. "You saw them yourself, didn't you?" she asked, turning frightened eyes upon me. Then for the next mile we all compared notes on what we had seen of the details of the outfit, and we were all in harmony as to many of the things we saw.

"Well," mother finally said, "I guess they must have been two of the Nephites that wanted to stay on earth and not taste death till the Savior comes again. Why, that's it," she cried, turning to me, "and they are going to Bluff to be there for conference tomorrow."

Some men to whom I have related this story have laughed to scorn the idea of anything supernatural connected with it, and have put it all down to mirage. "It was a desert mirage," they have told me. And when I have said that in all the desert mirages I had ever seen, they took the form and appearance of water, they have answered: "Oh well, what you saw was the reflection of some outfit somewhere."

And thus I leave it. And I am still waiting for the answer to the mystery and I am confident that some day I shall know that answer. But I solemnly declare to all men that what I have set down here is absolutely true, whether it was mirage, or some other force which created the glittering, moving picture we saw on that bright fall morning many years ago.

(Heart Throbs of the West, by Kate B. Carter. Daughters of Utah Pioneers. 1941. Vol. 3, pgs. 355-357.)

Chapter Fifty-Seven

Mrs. Fisher's Voice Was Restored

Mrs. Irvin Fisher

Oh, I'm seventy-two. I've been married going on fifty-two years. And I've lived in Utah all my life. I was born in Utah, and lived here all my life. But I had a real hard trial in my life, on account of which I whispered one third of my life. And the other two-thirds it was hard to talk. Because I had to use so much force, you know, to talk. And Mother took me to doctors and had me blessed by wonderful men, and I never got one bit of help from them. And I thought there was no hope; yet I got a blessing from a patriarch in 1899, and he told me of a great work that I was to do. And I thought that would be in another life and not this one. So I said, "Grandma, that can't come true." She says, "Oh, yes it can, every bit of it," she says. "I know what our Heavenly Father can do." She says, "He can bless you, and I'm going to pray for you as I've never prayed in my life."

And so she started right in to praying, and she prayed. And she prayed one month, and I thought maybe she'd get weak. And she prayed another month; and then she prayed another month. And when that month was up and it was just the last day, a knock came at my door. And I went to that door and pulled the curtain up a little way and saw it was a man with a gray beard and right white hair. A little frocktail coat and dark pants and a light shirt. I knew he couldn't hear my whispers, so I took hold of his hand and brought him into the house, because it came to me, "He's a Nephite of the living God! Let him in quick or he'll be gone!" And I knew it was one.

And then I set him down and he says, "Go get the dear old lady," he says, "that has prayed three solid months for your blessing." So I went and brought Grandma into this room, and she began to cry: "I've lived to be eighty-eight years old to behold a Nephite of the living God! "Ah," she said, "how wonderful!" I kissed her on the forehead and whispered, "Don't cry." And then I asked him if he'd like a glass of milk. And he said, "You can go and pray." And I went into the other room to pray. When I came back then he told me he had a prayer to offer that no human being had ever heard or ever would hear because it was given to him in Heaven. But he says, "It'll be literally fulfilled, every word of it." And I says, "Oh, I'm glad!" He said, "Set right down here." And I set right down by him. And he put his right hand on my head, and his left hand on my throat, and I shouted "Hosanna to God!"

The feeling that filled my soul! I pray that the ones that are listening to this will be thrilled with the same feeling. And then he blessed me; he blessed our home. Then he bid us goodbye and we went right out onto the porch — I took Grandma right with me. And he walked out of the gate just as spry as a young man, and walked along. When he came to the big gate, he didn't disappear, but he went right out of sight. He wasn't in the fields nor along the road nor any place. So I set Grandma down and ran where I could see along this road a mile and a half; and no signs of him. And I said to a lady, "Did you see a man pass here?" She said, "If a butterfly'd a-went by, I could a-seen it." She says, "There was no man passed here." So then I made myself quite contented.

And I pray with all my heart that the one that hears this will know that I testify unto it, and it is true as the sun rises in the east and sets in the west. And I've never whispered once since I got it. Never since my blessing, I've never whispered once. Nobody is going to realize what a great joy I get, being able to sing, to holler, to laugh, and make a noise. And I thank God with all my heart for this wonderful experience in my life. Amen! *(The Three Nephites, by Hector Haight Lee. The University of New Mexico. 1949. pgs. 140-142.)*

Chapter Fifty-Eight

Four Hundred Lamanites

Orson Pratt

There is one thing which has not yet been fulfilled, and which we must fulfill before Zion is redeemed. I will read it — "Behold, saith the Father, I will bring the fullness of my Gospel from among them, and then I will remember my covenant which I have made unto my people, O House of Israel, and I will bring my Gospel unto them." Now then, we are here in this land, the House of Israel are scattered all around us, some in the Great Basin, some in Arizona, some in Idaho, some in Colorado, some in Montana, some in one place, some in another; I refer to the American Indians, all remnants of Joseph and belonging to the House of Israel. They have become very degraded in consequence of the apostasy and wickedness of their ancient fathers. This people — the Latter-day Saints, before they can ever return to build up the waste place of Zion and receive their inheritances in Jackson County, Missouri, have got to exert themselves to bring the remnants of Joseph to a knowledge of the truth. We have not made any very great exertions in this direction unto the present time. The Lord has given us time since He brought the fullness of the Gospel from among the Gentiles to lay a foundation so that we could commence this missionary work in behalf of and among the remnants of Joseph. We have got the foundation laid, we have succeeded in building many cities, towns, villages, etc., for some four hundred miles north and south; we have got our farms fenced and our water ditches dug, and we have begun to prosper in the land, so that now, I think, is the time for us to wake up our minds in relation to the scattered remnants of the House of Israel." "Behold, then I will remember my covenant which I have made unto my people, O House of Israel, and I will bring my Gospel unto them."

It seems that the Lord is working among that people, and that he is determined this prophecy shall be fulfilled whether we take it in hand or not. What do my ears hear? What do we all hear? Messengers are visiting these wild tribes in the basin, and in the regions round about hundreds of miles apart. These messengers come to them, and they speak in their own language in great plainness, and tell them what to do; they tell them to repent of their sins and to be baptized for the remission thereof; tell them also to cease roaming over the country and to cultivate the land; tell them to go to the Elders of this Church and receive the ordinances under their hands.

Who are these messengers? Read the Book of Mormon and you will find what God promised to do for the remnants of Joseph fourteen hundred years ago, about the time that most of them were becoming wicked and corrupt. The Lord said when their record should come forth in the latter days that He would send His messengers to them, and among these messengers He mentioned three persons who lived some eighteen hundred years ago, three of the Twelve who were chosen on this land. The Lord made a promise to these three that they should administer as holy messengers in the latter days, for and in behalf of the remnants of the House of Israel, which should fall into a low and degraded condition in consequence of the great wickedness and apostasy of their ancient fathers; that they should be instruments in His hands in bringing these remnants to the knowledge of the truth. We hear that these messengers have come, not in one instance alone, but in many instances. Already we have heard of some fourteen hundred Indians, and I do not know but more, who have been baptized. Ask them why they have come so many hundred miles to find the Elders of the Church, and they will reply: "Such a person came to us, he spoke in our language, instructed us and told us what to do, and we have come in order to comply with his requirements." *(Journal of Discourses 17:299-300. Feb. 7, 1875.)*

Chapter Fifty-Nine

Three Nephites Rescued Us

Terri Steineckert Brinkerhoff

It had been a beautiful weekend that February of 1979. The snow had been pristine — pure and sparkling in the stillness of winter's icy bite. What glorious sights we had beheld as my husband and I celebrated our 7th wedding anniversary snowmobiling all around Island Park, Idaho — a small rural blink just outside of Yellowstone National Park. We had left our four small children in the care of a neighbor at our home in Pocatello and taken off for our anniversary vacation.

We had rented snowmobiles and complete snowsuits from a little rental outlet and spent the day frolicking in the crystal grandeur. It was clear and crisp with perfect blue skies overhead arching down to hug the earth in its wintery shroud. Snowball fights, talking and walking hand-in-hand along the banks of a river, meandering along unknown trails, and zipping over hills and meadows on our fast machines breaking the silence with the high-pitched whine of the engine; it was beautiful and exhilarating, and we loved every minute of it.

As our day drew to a close, we returned our borrowed vehicles and snowsuits and jumped into our heated station wagon for the 2-hour journey home. Our children and our dinner would be awaiting our arrival and we were eager to tell them about all we had seen and done. It was great to get away, but how we had missed them, too.

A little ways down the road my husband, Neil, suggested we take a brief side trip. He was a Sales Rep in this area and sometimes had traveled this route calling on his accounts. He had previously discovered a waterfall nearby and thought I might enjoy seeing it in this wonderful wintery fairyland setting. At a seemingly unlikely spot, just a little wider gap between tree-trunk fence posts, he turned off the main highway and headed into a thicket of trees. The road was icy and snowpacked but still had been plowed, so we never once anticipated the challenges that would soon confront us.

As we proceeded down this lonely and isolated country lane, heading farther and farther away from civilization, traffic, and humanity, we felt a growing sense of alarm. The road quickly narrowed and the snow suddenly deepened. We had passed the point the snowplow had cleared and before we knew it we were driving our car through virgin snowdrifts. It was deep; well above the bumper on the front of the car, and as we inched our way along it became increasingly more difficult to steer or maneuver. We dared not stop for fear of becoming stuck — we needed to keep the momentum to continue rolling forward in search of a place to turn around. We struggled to prevent sliding off the road and into the gullies that bordered its edges, since we were on a sheet of ice under the blanket of white that surrounded us.

As Neil became more and more aware of the predicament we found ourselves in, he began to panic. The farther we went the more alarmed and upset he became. We suspected we were miles from the next town and night was rapidly approaching. We did not have food with us; and our warm snowsuits, boots, gloves, and hats had just been rented and returned. The sweatshirts and tennis shoes we were wearing would hardly accommodate hiking back to the main road. And, we were out of gas!

There was no sign of life anywhere. No telephone poles, no spirals of smoke from a nearby chimney, no road signs or markers, no evidence of life at all. And after many miles and an eternity of minutes, there was still no sign of the waterfall we had sought. Suddenly our glorious winter wonderland became frightening. Cold. Lifeless. Dead. The stillness was the silence of loneliness and impending doom; of danger lurking in the dark shadows.

Neil fought the steering wheel with white knuckles, clenched teeth and shaking shoulders. He cried as he moaned and wailed that we would surely freeze to death if we did, indeed, run out of gas. Maybe one of us could try to go for help, but which direction? With nightfall coming on, would we get lost? Would we freeze or would wild and hungry animals prey upon us? We might never see our children again or live to raise them. We were so far off the beaten path that we might not even be found until spring — Oh, please spare our families the agony of not knowing the fate that had befallen us. He gripped the wheel ever tighter and sobbed in fear for our lives.

Alas, a little clearing! The tip of a rustic wooden sign popped above the snow, an indication that this was an obscure intersection with another road angling off to the left deep under the snow drifts. Slowly ever so slightly, we attempted to execute a wide turn so we could go back out the way we had come in. It had been far too risky to try to just reverse our direction and back out, but now, if we could just turn around.

Crash!! The car lost its traction on the icy buildup of snow two feet beneath the powder that hampered our progress. We could not see the ditch that lay in the corner on the right where the two roads met, but we felt it as our right rear wheel slid off the road into it. Now we were really stuck. Alone. Cold. Hungry. Tired. Lost. Scared. And, nearly out of gas. Oh, why did we ever leave the security of that straight and narrow highway that would have led us directly home? Why were we exploring unknown roads when the things that mattered most to us were waiting for us at home?

Neil jumped out of the car to assess our predicament. Instinct compelled me to begin honking the horn on our car. I don't know why — I just thought if there did happen to be anyone within hearing distance it might help. But, about the third time I honked, Neil reached into the car and grabbed me, pulling me out into the snow. "Quit that!" he screamed. "Do you want to cause an avalanche?"

That stopped me cold. I hadn't considered that possibility. I guess there were a lot of possible realities I hadn't wanted to face up to that point. The whole time Neil had been so panic stricken, I had remained calm and kept the faith. I just didn't feel in my heart that we were in that much jeopardy and I thought it just a little silly that he was so hysterical. But, try as I did to comfort and reassure him, he kept reminding me that I was the one not facing the reality of the precarious situation we were in.

My thought process changed gears at that point. Okay, we were stranded. There was no help in sight. And, we would be in serious danger of freezing once the sun went down, and already the shadows were lengthening. What could we do? What resources did we have? We rapidly eliminated any hope of food or warmth as we assessed the supplies we had in the back of the car. The only thing back there was a set of tire chains and they couldn't keep us warm or provide any nutritional value.

Wait! If we could somehow get the chains onto the back tires, maybe that would give us the traction we needed to get out of the hole and back onto the road. It was worth a try! We knelt together at the rear of the car and began untangling the web of chains when a sudden warm peace came over me. I wasn't sure if the chains would work or not, but I knew something that would. Gently and calmly I reached out and took hold of Neil's hands. They were cold and quivering, but stilled considerably as I held them tightly. The words of a prayer formed on my lips and the sound of my heartfelt plea ascended heavenward through the bitter cold.

I explained to Heavenly Father exactly where we were and why, and how we had come to be there. I reminded Him that we had four very young children at home whom we wanted very much to raise and influence and watch grow up. I expressed a willingness to devote my life to serving Him wherever and however He needed me, and then I asked with all the intensity of my soul that He might give us the wisdom and direction that we needed at that time to know how to best cope with our predicament. We prayed for our children and our families to be comforted, and not alarmed at our delayed homecoming. We prayed that searchers would be guided to find us before it was too late. And we prayed for peace, courage, and inspiration. "Please, Father in Heaven, please send us the help that we need. Please. Please?. . ."

As I closed our prayer I heard the hum of a fly or mosquito buzzing overhead. Opening my eyes, I shook my head at the absurdity of that idea — it was 17 degrees outside. Surely there weren't any pests of that nature now. Wait. There it was again. Louder. Closer. Familiar. SNOWMOBILES!!!

I jumped back into the car again and started honking for all I was worth. We had one chance of being found, and I wasn't going to blow it by sitting silently or idly by. Wishing I knew Morse Code or some kind of SOS, I just kept honking. Neil sat transfixed in the snow just beyond the open car door. Doubting our "luck" or good fortune, he recognized he was powerless to stop me at that point nonetheless, so he let me just keep on honking. I was determined to get the attention of whoever it might be. I never once considered what type of people it might be, out there alone, so far from anything or anyone else.

In a matter of just seconds, although it felt like an eternity, over the ridge just ahead of us crested three men riding on two snowmobiles. I noticed a dead fox bouncing on the back of the machine with the single rider and assumed they were poachers being so far out in such a remote area. Remembering back though, I don't remember seeing any guns. They had long-ish hair and beards and reminded me of "hippies" at first glance. Their clothes were rugged and worn, lacking color or description, and yet there was something about their faces. The radiance of color after all day out riding in the sun almost made their faces glow, and there was a kindness, a compassion, an understanding or something about their eyes. I couldn't quite put my finger on it. But I didn't question it either. These men were our saviours and it didn't matter right then who they were, what they were doing there, or where they had come from!

They came right up to us and sized up our situation as they approached. I finally stopped honking the horn and got out of the car once again to join my husband. Greeting us briefly, they explained that they had just been ready to call it a day and head back to town (about 25 miles away we learned), when they had suddenly and unexplainedly begun having engine trouble with one of the snowmobiles. Opting to take the "old deserted highway" instead of the more rugged trails through the forest, they had been heading our direction the first time I had honked. Hearing me, they had concluded exactly what I had hoped, and made a bee-line right for us, sensing that someone was in trouble.

We briefly discussed our options with them. We could remain where we were and they could go get help. We would try to ride with them (5 of us on 2 machines) into town. Or, they could try to get the car out of the ditch and turned around. Right!

But, before we could protest or even respond, two of these men (who were not particularly strong or muscular, just average build it appeared) jumped off their machines and came over to the car. Pausing, and looking at each other as if it would give them strength, one walked to the front of the car and the other got down into the ditch where he could reach the rear of the station wagon. Together they rocked the car back and forth a couple of times and then seemed to jump it, or almost pick it up, and place it right where it needed to go — right in the middle of the road! Neil and I just looked on incredulously. These guys were a lot stronger than they looked! One of them suggested we get back into the car and he would follow us back out to the main highway just to make sure we made it okay. The other two men would wait there with the faltering snowmobile to spare it from undue usage until the first man returned and then they would continue on in their own direction.

On our way out we tried to follow the ruts our tires had made in the snow coming in. Why blaze a trail a second time when we could just retrace our steps? It was difficult, but we felt so much safer just knowing someone was watching out for us, and that help was within sight. What a comfort it was to look out the back window and see the spray shooting up from his snowmobile as he sped to keep up with us, and to see his smile or wave of encouragement. It seemed to take hardly any time at all before we were back to the main road, with traffic speeding past in both directions. We knew a town was less than 1/2 hour away and we felt sure we had enough gas to get us that far. We felt confident, and ever-so-grateful.

When we finally got safely onto the plowed part of our misadventure detour, we stopped and got out of the car. We wanted to thank our gracious benefactor. As Neil reached out to shake his hand, he paused and took $5.00 from his wallet and offered it to the man. The man drew his hand away quickly and refused to take our money. "We have sufficient for our needs," he told us, and then explained that they were there to help and did not need compensation other than the satisfaction of being of service. Then, he got on his snowmobile and headed back to join his companions we had left about 10 miles away.

We had stopped about 1/2 mile from where the trees became dense. The whole way out of the forest, we had been able to watch our new friend as he followed us. No matter how the road had twisted or turned, we could see him, see his tracks, and the spray from his machine. Now, getting into the car and approaching the highway, we looked back across the open meadow for one final wave good-bye, but he was gone! The man, the snowmobile, even the tracks! Vanished. As if they had never existed except in our imaginations.

Neil and I looked at each other. Goose bumps popped out all over my body, and yet physically I was warm. I started to cry. We stared at each other a long time. And we stared behind us where he should have been visible. After quite a while we both nodded our heads and at the same time said, "Those were the Three Nephites . . .", and through the spirit, we knew it was true.

Signed: Terri Brinkerhoff
November 12, 1992

Chapter Sixty

Old Mining Town Visitor

Wilford H. "Buck" Farley

I was almost 10 years old. My family lived in the small coal mining community of Upland, located along the Elkhorn River on U.S. Route 52 in McDowell County, West Virginia.

My father was mine foreman for Upland Coal & Coke Company and also was part owner of a small mine with another foreman, Mr. Yates.

It was a Saturday afternoon in the summer of 1946. My dad had taken me to the company store. I don't recall why we were there. I don't remember buying anything but ice cream. As we walked out the door, my attention was drawn to an old man walking toward us from around the curve in the highway that ran through town. He was not at all familiar to me and I knew everyone in town.

The thing that impressed me at the time was that he sought out my dad. I saw that although his clothing was less than immaculate, he was extremely clean with a flawless complexion. He had very white hair that was thin at the front and blue eyes that were a clear blue. He was about 5'-7" tall and appeared to be in his seventies.

As he and my dad began a conversation, I went into the store park area to play. I noticed from the park that the old man talked only to my dad.

After about twenty minutes, dad called for me and said it was time to go home. The old man said 'goodbye' and instead of going down the road he walked toward the railroad but went around the building where only a small platform existed that hung over the river bank. It was there to give access to store offices that were closed for the weekend.

As we started to leave, dad said, "there's something else I should ask him." So we hurried to the corner of the store. As we turned the corner, we expected to see him leaning on the railing because there was nowhere else to go. However, he was not there. He had vanished! He wasn't in the river nor did he cross the bridge to the railroad. He had just vanished!

Dad was very quiet on the way home and never said much about his conversation to me. However, dad ordered a new Oldsmobile (cars were finally available after the war) which came in

October. We started going to church in Bluefield every Sunday. Once in the morning for Sunday School and Priesthood and in the evening for Sacrament. This was eighteen miles through the West Virginia hills twice each Sunday. A big change for our family. Dad was ordained to the priesthood and in June of 1947, we made a trip west and mom and dad were sealed in the Salt Lake Temple and we were sealed to them in the Logan Temple.

After returning home, dad became a leader in the branch and later was instrumental in forming the Welch Branch. When he retired from the mines, we moved to Riverside, California and at the time of his death he was Ward Clerk.

I don't know if dad was told not to share what he was told. The only time I ever heard him speak of it was when he told mom once, "I wonder if the old man that came to me at the company store was one of the Three Nephites or John the Baptist."

Now that I'm older, I wished I had pressed him for details. I'm not sure I would have been told. All I have are memories of what happened and maybe that's all I was to know.

I'm not sure who he was but I do know that he was special. I know that whatever he told my dad, it changed his life and I grew up with church responsibilities and callings from a young age that I may never have had, if the "old visitor" had not come to Upland, West Virginia in the summer of 1946. *(Submitted by Wilford H. "Buck" Farley, Provo, Utah, 1992.)*

Conclusion

It is our hope that after you have had the opportunity of reading and pondering these wonderful experiences of other Latter-day Saints, that your testimony has been enlarged and strengthened. The abundance of spiritual experiences in the Church is always a source of positive, celestial motivation. We found ourselves captivated by the very existence of these records and evidences. As we spent many hundreds of hours researching, gathering and compiling Three Nephite encounters, our appreciation for the Gospel of Jesus Christ expanded and our hearts became full.

Searching the many libraries, archives and other areas which contained these plain and precious writings, fostered a greater understanding of the importance of properly documenting our own life history and family experiences. Many of the records and texts were out of print and many others are simply unattainable. Accuracy was a prime motivation in our efforts to present this valuable information, and for that purpose we have documented and credited the source material to the best of our knowledge.

Some individuals will label these heartfelt testimonies and sacred experiences as "folklore" and doubt their authenticity and also the motives of the believer. However, this does not diminish the devout belief and the proper illustration of gospel principles such as faith and prayer and miracles and gifts of the spirit which are very much in abundance today. To be able to read first person accounts of angelic visitations of Christ's disciples in our time is a unique opportunity not afforded to disingenuous persons who attempt to minimize its importance.

That which is instructional and faith promoting to some, is described as "myth" by others. In a categorical sense, the many testaments to the Three Nephites have been classified into six categories with six related elements by Hector Haight Lee of the University of New Mexico. After an exhaustive study of 150 narratives involving the Three Nephites, Lee and his group presented the following analysis and breakdown.

1.   A Nephite requests food. (12%)
2.   A Nephite heals the sick. (11%)
3.   A Nephite delivers a spiritual message. (34%)
4.   A Nephite rescues and gives physical help. (14%)

5.   A Nephite transports with miraculous speed. (4%)

6.   A Nephite suddenly disappears. (25%)

Some of the above elements were combined and found in duality in some of the experiences. The biggest number of experiences portray the Three Nephites as delivering and bringing a spiritual message which, as in all cases, is in keeping with their divine charge as missionaries of Christ.

We also learn that the Three Nephites may predict events and prophecy, may know or anticipate a person's thoughts and troubles, and may also heal the sick and give physical aid to the needy. The Nephites can give advice and helpful information, can request food, drink, rest and lodging; may appear suddenly and disappear just as quickly. The three have a tremendous knowledge of the Gospel of Jesus Christ and may bless and spiritually uplift those they come into contact with. We have learned all of this through the personal testimonies found within the covers of this volume. We discover that these are personality traits which we should all emulate and pattern our lives after. The Three Nephites were specially chosen by the Savior as missionary role models for us all.

The reality of the Three Nephites is more than simple legend, myth or folklore; much more. We not only have the scriptural record of the Savior's pronouncement, decree and blessing upon the three disciples, but we have hundreds of eye witness testimonies of their celestial endeavors here on the earth among the saints.

The Three Nephites involvement in current world affairs is unknown to us at present. We do not know of all of the total involvement in the establishment of Zion on this continent and throughout the world. Nor do we know of their participation in the inspired discovery of this land we call America. Our duty is to continually study the scriptures which contain the word of God, obey the commandments and be true to our holy covenants; looking with an eye single to the glory of God and all His righteousness.

About the Authors

Douglas and Jewel Beardall have both served as full-time missionaries. Sister Beardall served in the Frankfurt, West German Mission and Brother Beardall served

in the Chicago, Illinois Mission.

After receiving their formal educations at Brigham Young University, they were married in the Salt Lake Temple by Elder LeGrand Richards.

Douglas and Jewel have also written and published *The Miracle of Love, For Missionaries Only!, Cookbook for All Seasons, Passage to Light, The Missionary Kit, Death and the LDS Family, Mormon Money Matters,* and various articles which have been published in national magazines, trade journals and periodicals including *The Ensign* magazine.

The Beardall's work in publishing has taken their residence to Southern California, Southern Nevada, and Utah where they now reside with their four children; Jeff, Holly, Jennifer, and Scott.